W9-CPB-904

OPPOSING
VIEWPOINTS®
SERIES

Labor Unions

Other Books of Related Interest:

Opposing Viewpoints Series

America in the Twenty-First Century

Illegal Immigration

Working Women

At Issue Series

Does Outsourcing Harm America?

"Congress shall make no law . . . abridging the freedom of speech, or of the press."

First Amendment to the U.S. Constitution

The basic foundation of our democracy is the First Amendment guarantee of freedom of expression. The Opposing Viewpoints series is dedicated to the concept of this basic freedom and the idea that it is more important to practice it than to enshrine it.

Labor Unions

Viqi Wagner, Book Editor

GREENHAVEN PRESS

An imprint of Thomson Gale, a part of The Thomson Corporation

THOMSON
™
GALE

Detroit • New York • San Francisco • New Haven, Conn. • Waterville, Maine • London

THOMSON
★ ™
GALE

Christine Nasso, *Publisher*
Elizabeth Des Chenes, *Managing Editor*

© 2008 The Gale Group.

Star logo is a trademark and Gale and Greenhaven Press are registered trademarks used herein under license.

For more information, contact:
Greenhaven Press
27500 Drake Rd.
Farmington Hills, MI 48331-3535
Or you can visit our Internet site at http://www.gale.com

LIBRARY OF CONGRESS CATALOGING-IN-PUBLICATION DATA

Labor unions / Viqi Wagner, book editor.
    p. cm. -- Opposing Viewpoints
    Includes bibliographical references and index.
    ISBN-13: 978-0-7377-3822-3 (hardcover)
    ISBN-13: 978-0-7377-3823-0 (pbk.)
    1. Labor unions--Juvenile literature. I. Wagner, Viqi, 1953-
    HD6483.5.L33 2008
    331.88--dc22
                                                                2007036345

ISBN-10: 0-7377-3822-7 (hardcover)
ISBN-10: 0-7377-3823-5 (pbk.)

Printed in the United States of America
10 9 8 7 6 5 4 3 2 1

Contents

Chapter 3: Should Wal-Mart Unionize?

Chapter 4: What Is the Future of Organized Labor?

Why Consider Opposing Viewpoints?

> *"The only way in which a human being can make some approach to knowing the whole of a subject is by hearing what can be said about it by persons of every variety of opinion and studying all modes in which it can be looked at by every character of mind. No wise man ever acquired his wisdom in any mode but this."*
>
> *John Stuart Mill*

In our media-intensive culture it is not difficult to find differing opinions. Thousands of newspapers and magazines and dozens of radio and television talk shows resound with differing points of view. The difficulty lies in deciding which opinion to agree with and which "experts" seem the most credible. The more inundated we become with differing opinions and claims, the more essential it is to hone critical reading and thinking skills to evaluate these ideas. Opposing Viewpoints books address this problem directly by presenting stimulating debates that can be used to enhance and teach these skills. The varied opinions contained in each book examine many different aspects of a single issue. While examining these conveniently edited opposing views, readers can develop critical thinking skills such as the ability to compare and contrast authors' credibility, facts, argumentation styles, use of persuasive techniques, and other stylistic tools. In short, the Opposing Viewpoints series is an ideal way to attain the higher-level thinking and reading skills so essential in a culture of diverse and contradictory opinions.

In addition to providing a tool for critical thinking, Opposing Viewpoints books challenge readers to question their own strongly held opinions and assumptions. Most people form their opinions on the basis of upbringing, peer pressure, and personal, cultural, or professional bias. By reading carefully balanced opposing views, readers must directly confront new ideas as well as the opinions of those with whom they disagree. This is not to simplistically argue that everyone who reads opposing views will—or should—change his or her opinion. Instead, the series enhances readers' understanding of their own views by encouraging confrontation with opposing ideas. Careful examination of others' views can lead to the readers' understanding of the logical inconsistencies in their own opinions, perspective on why they hold an opinion, and the consideration of the possibility that their opinion requires further evaluation.

Evaluating Other Opinions

To ensure that this type of examination occurs, Opposing Viewpoints books present all types of opinions. Prominent spokespeople on different sides of each issue as well as well-known professionals from many disciplines challenge the reader. An additional goal of the series is to provide a forum for other, less-known, or even unpopular viewpoints. The opinion of an ordinary person who has had to make the decision to cut off life support from a terminally ill relative, for example, may be just as valuable and provide just as much insight as a medical ethicist's professional opinion. The editors have two additional purposes in including these less-known views. One, the editors encourage readers to respect others' opinions—even when not enhanced by professional credibility. It is only by reading or listening to and objectively evaluating others' ideas that one can determine whether they are worthy of consideration. Two, the inclusion of such viewpoints encourages the important critical thinking skill of objectively evaluating an author's credentials and bias. This evaluation will illuminate an author's reasons for taking a particular stance on an issue and will aid in readers' evaluation of the author's ideas.

It is our hope that these books will give readers a deeper understanding of the issues debated and an appreciation of the complexity of even seemingly simple issues when good and honest people disagree. This awareness is particularly important in a democratic society such as ours in which people enter into public debate to determine the common good. Those with whom one disagrees should not be regarded as enemies but rather as people whose views deserve careful examination and may shed light on one's own.

Thomas Jefferson once said that "difference of opinion leads to inquiry, and inquiry to truth." Jefferson, a broadly educated man, argued that "if a nation expects to be ignorant and free . . . it expects what never was and never will be." As individuals and as a nation, it is imperative that we consider the opinions of others and examine them with skill and discernment. The Opposing Viewpoints series is intended to help readers achieve this goal.

David L. Bender and Bruno Leone,
Founders

Introduction

> *"Our employers have changed, our industries have changed, and the world has certainly changed, but the labor movement's structure and culture have sadly stayed the same."*
>
> *—Service Employees International Union president Andy Stern, 2004*

The American labor movement has experienced two periods of great upheaval and disunity, each of which mirrored a paradigm shift in the structure of the U.S. economy. Each period was marked by dramatic change in where and how and by whom goods were produced. In each period, organized labor faced sharp declines in numbers and influence which led to predictions of its obsolescence if not its extinction.

The first upheaval coincided with the rise of factories and assembly-line production in the late 1800s and early 1900s. The iron and steel, mining, and automobile industries needed blue-collar labor, not the (more costly) skilled craftsmen of the pre-industrial era who resisted working for wages paid by monopolistic companies. But organized craftsmen could not compete with waves of immigrants willing to work for less and accept poorer working conditions. By the 1920s, craft unions and labor leaders were forced to accept the spread of factories and the inevitability of working for wages. The labor movement turned its focus to organizing industrial workers and securing for them as large a share of the wealth they were producing as possible.

Labor responded to the industrial revolution with new solidarity: Strong leaders such as Samuel Gompers and John

L. Lewis rallied workers to the American Federation of Labor (AFL) and the Congress of Industrial Occupations (CIO), respectively. Labor also was backed by new legislative protections, above all, the National Labor Relations Act of 1935 (or Wagner Act), which guaranteed workers the right to join labor unions and to bargain collectively with company management. And labor adopted new strategies: primarily, grass-roots organizing of immigrant and poor communities and working to overcome employers' deep, historically violent distrust of unions.

The transformation worked. Between 1935 and 1940, union membership rose from 3.8 to 9 million. Union growth continued through World War II. Through the 1950s and 1960s, led by the merged AFL-CIO, the union movement enjoyed unprecedented influence, as former secretary of labor Robert Reich explains:

> More than a third of the American workforce was unionized, and wages and benefits of most workers rose steadily. Organized labor's clout during those years reflected the new realities of mass production. In order to achieve huge economies of scale, major industries became dominated by a few giant producers—three major automakers, five chemical manufacturers, six steel makers, a handful of airlines, and so on. . . . Most blue-collar jobs in them were boiled down to certain predictable steps, done over and over.
>
> The mass production system was an ideal environment for organized labor. Since mass production depended on predictability, a strike or work stoppage could wreak havoc. Hence, management was eager to bargain. On the other hand, because big companies in each major industry didn't really compete much with each other, they willingly accepted the terms of the same industrywide labor contracts. . . . Moreover, labor contracts could be based on industrywide job classifications and work rules.

In this prosperous age, union members saw tangible returns on the dues they paid. Union negotiators won contracts that included not only higher wages but nonwage benefits such as paid holidays and vacations, health insurance, and pension plans, so-called fringe benefits that union workers and nonunion workers alike soon came to expect as standard parts of employers' compensation packages. They also enjoyed job security: Most union workers could reasonably expect to work for a single employer throughout their career, support a family on their wages, and retire on a company pension. But as Reich laments, "That was then."

The second period of great upheaval and disunity in the American labor movement is occurring now, reflecting another paradigm shift in the structure of the U.S. economy that began in the 1970s and has brought organized labor to its knees.

Today, only 7.4 percent of private-sector workers are unionized. In contrast to the era of new legislation protecting union activity, today twenty-two states enforce so-called right-to-work laws, which state that new employees of a unionized company do not have to join that union or pay dues to get or keep their jobs. (Union contracts must cover nonunion employees as well, so right-to-work laws effectively reduce the incentive to join unions.) Today strikes are infrequent and more likely to fail; more employers simply hire nonunion replacements or use aggressive unionbusting tactics such as lockouts when union workers do walk out (or, increasingly, even threaten to walk out). In 2005, several large dissident members of the AFL-CIO broke away to form a rival labor federation, Change to Win (CTW), further eroding union solidarity.

Just as it did a century ago, the turnaround in labor unions' fortunes reflects a paradigm shift in the U.S. economy and dramatic change in where and how and by whom goods are produced. Four broad trends describe this change, according to labor policy expert Robert P. Hunter:

Global competition and deregulation in traditionally union-ized industries ... including the trucking, railroad, and air-line industries. Deregulation has brought greater competi-tion to these industries not only domestically but also from abroad. . . .

Changes in the American economy and workforce demographics. . . . The rising number of illegal immigrants who, fearing deportation, are disinclined to protest substan-dard employment conditions, much less become involved in a union organizing campaign. The rapidly expanding con-tingent workforce—composed mostly of women, temporary workers, and part-time employees—has also proven to be difficult for unions to organize. Additionally, shifts in the American job market from the stagnant manufacturing sec-tor to an expanding service sector and the creation of many new largely white-collar and technical occupations. . . .

Federal employment law supplanting traditional union roles. . . . Congress has passed a number of new laws and mandates designed to combat employment discrimination . . . establish safe and healthy workplaces, provide family and medical leave, give workers notice for plant closings, and much more. The trend has been for government to assume responsibility for more and more of the things traditionally advocated and protected by unions.

Today's workers are less interested in unionization. . . . The current generation of workers comes largely from house-holds where there are no union workers to serve as models. . . . [They are more sympathetic to business, and] desire unions that are willing to cooperate with manage-ment rather than confront it.

Union supporters dispute Hunter's last reason, placing more blame on wholesale corporate downsizing, outsourcing, and relocation of manufacturing facilities overseas, where la-bor is plentiful and cheap. The problem, they say, is not that American workers are leaving unions; the problem is that jobs are leaving American workers. Indisputably, organized labor must contend with immense pressure for change in the U.S. workplace, and as it did a century ago, transform itself if it is to survive. The challenges facing labor unions, and responses to those challenges, are debated in *Opposing Viewpoints: Labor Unions* in the following chapters: "What Is the Status of U.S. Labor Unions?" "How Have Immigration and Globalization Affected Labor Unions?" "Should Wal-Mart Unionize?" and "What Is the Future of Organized Labor?" The decisions of employers, workers, governments, and unions will determine the shape of tomorrow's workplace.

CHAPTER 1

What Is the Status of U.S. Labor Unions?

Chapter Preface

The Bureau of Labor Statistics (BLS) of the U.S. Department of Labor is the federal government's principal fact-finding agency in the field of labor economics and statistics. Its annual report, *Union Members Summary*, compiled from Census Bureau population studies, is the most widely referenced source of information on union participation in the United States. In addition to counting people who belong to a union (or whose jobs are covered by a union contract even if they themselves are not union members), the summary breaks down union membership by industry and occupation, age, sex, race, state, and other criteria.

The main finding of the *Union Members Summary* released in January 2007 is unambiguous: Overall union membership in the United States fell by 326,000 people in 2006, from 12.5 to 12.0 percent of American workers, roughly 15.4 million people. This finding is not surprising—union membership has fallen every year since the BLS began compiling comparable data in 1983, when 20.1 percent of American workers were union members. Now as then, union membership is higher among men than women (13.0 percent versus 10.9 percent) and highest in the private sector among transportation and utilities and construction industries. North Carolina and South Carolina report the lowest rates of union membership, New York and Hawaii the highest. Union membership is highest among full-time workers forty-five to sixty-four years old and, according to the report, "Black workers were more likely to be union members (14.5 percent) than were whites (11.7 percent), Asians (10.4 percent), or Hispanics (9.8 percent)."

But the finding that *overall* union membership dropped to 12.0 percent in 2006 is misleading. This generalization obscures the surprising fact that there are two unionization trends occurring in the United States: Union membership among public-sector occupations—primarily local government workers such as teachers, police officers, and firefighters—is *growing* as private-sector unionization falls. Today, 37.3 percent of education and library workers and 34.7 percent of protective service workers are union members, even as the rate of unionization among private-sector industries has dropped to 7.4 percent, the lowest level since 1932.

The contributors to the following chapter debate the reasons for and meaning of these diverging trends and whether labor unions benefit or exploit the U.S. worker and the taxpayer.

> "Not only did the share of workers who were union members fall from 25 percent in 1977 to 14 percent by 1997 (a decline of 44 percent), but the total number of union members also decreased by nearly 4 million between these years."

Labor Unions Are in Decline

Robert E. Baldwin

In the mid-1950s, 36 percent of the U.S. labor force were union members. From that peak, union membership began a decline that continues unabated: Today, only 12 percent of American workers are unionized. In this viewpoint, economist Robert E. Baldwin argues that labor unions are not in decline because new technology is displacing human workers or corporations are outsourcing U.S. jobs to lower-paid workers overseas—according to his analysis, these trends affect union and nonunion jobs equally, so the overall proportion of union workers should be the same. Instead, Baldwin blames strong antiunion sentiment among U.S. workers and employers and effective antiunion policies in government. Robert E. Baldwin is Hilldale Professor of Economics Emeritus at the University of Wisconson-Madison and a former

Robert E. Baldwin, *The Decline of U.S. Labor Unions and the Role of Trade*. Washington, DC: Institute for International Economics, June 2003. Copyright © 2003 by the Institute for International Economics. Reproduced by permission.

consultant on trade matters to the U.S. Department of Labor, the World Bank, and the Organization for Economic Cooperation and Development.

As you read, consider the following questions:

1. According to Melvin Reder, cited by Baldwin, what rapidly growing categories of the labor force are less likely to unionize?
2. What three kinds of government activity have weakened labor unions, according to the author?
3. How has increased international trade affected "basically educated union workers" (workers with twelve or fewer years of education), in the author's view?

The American labor movement did not fare well during the last quarter of the 20th century. Not only did the share of workers who were union members fall from 25 percent in 1977 to 14 percent by 1997 (a decline of 44 percent), but the total number of union members also decreased by nearly 4 million between these years despite an overall increase in the number of jobs by more than 37 million. The extent of deunionization in the manufacturing sector was particularly dramatic, with the proportion of unionized workers falling from 38 percent in 1977 to 18 percent in 1997 (a decline of 53 percent). The only bright spot was in the public sector, where the proportion of unionized workers increased.

Why Have Labor Unions Declined?

Various explanations have been set forth to account for this deunionization trend in the private sector. In an article in a symposium on public and private unionization, Melvin Reder (1988) lists the following as the main causal factors cited by various researchers: (1) increased interarea competition, both domestic and international; (2) more rapid growth in certain categories of the labor force (e.g., women, southerners, white-collar workers) that are less favorable to unionization than others; (3) deregulation of transportation industries; (4) declining efforts of unions to recruit new members; (5) government activity that substitutes for union services (e.g., unemployment insurance and industrial accident insurance); (6) a decline in prounion attitudes among workers; and (7) increased employer resistance to unionization efforts.

In another contribution to this symposium, Richard Freeman (1988) also lists antiunion government policies—such as the actions of Ronald Reagan's administration in destroying the union representing U.S. air controllers in response to their strike in 1981—as among the possible causes of deunionization. He concludes that the main reason for the decline in U.S. private-sector unionization is increased management opposition to union organization, motivated by such profit-related factors as a rise in the union wage premium, increased foreign competition, and government deregulation policies. Still another factor frequently mentioned in recent years as contributing to the weakening of labor unions is the unskilled labor-displacing nature of new technology, including outsourcing.

There is, however, no general agreement among labor specialists concerning the relative importance of these various possible explanations. Initial research into the decline in union membership in the late 1970s and early 1980s stresses the importance of shifts in the composition of the labor force and the structure of production. Later studies de-emphasize this explanation, however, in part because these changes are themselves outcomes to be explained at a more fundamental level. Henry Farber and Alan Krueger (1992) conclude on the basis of survey data that virtually all of the decline in union membership from the 1970s to early 1990s was due to a decline in worker demand for union representation and that there was almost no change in the relative supply of union jobs. Of

Twenty-Five Years of Steady Decline

In 2006, 12.0 percent of employed wage and salary workers were union members, down from 12.5 percent a year earlier, the U.S. Department of Labor's Bureau of Labor Statistics reported [in January 2007]. The number of persons belonging to a union fell by 326,000 in 2006 to 15.4 million. The union membership rate has steadily declined from 20.1 percent in 1983, the first year for which comparable union data are available. Some highlights from the 2006 data are:

—Workers in the public sector had a union membership rate nearly five times that of private sector employees.

—Education, training, and library occupations had the highest unionization rate among all occupations, at 37 percent.

—The unionization rate was higher for men than for women.

—Black workers were more likely to be union members than were white, Asian, or Hispanic workers.

U.S. Department of Labor, "Union Members Summary,"
Bureau of Labor Statistics, January 25, 2007.

course, many of the same basic economic forces affecting employers' profit-oriented decisions could also affect workers' decisions about the desirability of union representation.

U.S. union leaders themselves place much of the blame for deunionization on the actions of American corporations. In their view, corporate America's aggressive efforts to increase profits have led to a variety of business actions and public policies designed to reduce labor costs by weakening unions' bargaining power. These corporate actions range from efforts aimed at preventing domestic unionization and at decertifying existing union representation to importing intermediate inputs rather than producing them domestically and establishing (or threatening to establish) their own outsourcing facilities in lower-wage countries. With respect to governmental policies, union leaders maintain that corporate America has used its greater political funding and lobbying capabilities to secure both domestic legislation weakening the right of workers to organize and international legislation reducing the bargaining power of organized labor by promoting agreements with other countries that expand trade and foreign direct investment without ensuring the enforcement of core labor rights internationally.

Offshore Business Is Not to Blame for Union Decline

[My 2003 study] describes the nature of the deunionization process during two decades, 1977–87 and 1987–97, both nationally and regionally. Then it focuses on one of the several suggested explanations for deunionization, namely, the increased openness of the United States to international trade. Utilizing microeconomic data collected as part of the U.S. government's annual Sample Census of Population, I [investigated] statistically whether the increased openness of the United States to international trade during these years affected the employment of union workers disproportionately compared with nonunion workers, that is, more adversely (or less beneficially) than would be expected from the relative importance for overall employment of these two groups of workers. If so, is it a major possible explanatory factor for deunionization?. . .

Some of the main findings: only about one-quarter of the total decline in the national rate of unionization between 1977 and 1987 and just one-tenth of the total decline in the 1987–97 period can be attributed to between-industries shifts in national employment shares from more unionized to less unionized industries, holding constant the within-industries unionization rates of all industries. Thus, declines in rates of unionization within industries, holding industry national employment shares constant, respectively explain (in an accounting sense) three-quarters and nine-tenths of the national deunionization during the first and second decades. Separating the changes in the national unionization rate in the manufacturing sector alone into these two components indicates an even greater role for the within-industries effect in accounting for deunionization during the two periods.

Between-industries shifts in shares of national manufacturing employment account for only 11 percent of the decrease in the unionization rate in manufacturing during the 1977–87 decade, compared with 89 percent due to within-industries changes in manufacturing unionization rates. During the 1987–97 period, between-industries shifts in manufacturing had the effect of increasing the rate of unionization. Moreover, gains in national employment shares by the U.S. southern and western regions served to reduce their overall unionization declines.

Although the significant change in imports and exports across almost all industries in both periods is a possible explanatory factor for the general decline in industry unionization rates, regression analysis indicates that increased international trade has not been the major factor in the decline. Factors other than changes in trade or in the other independent variables in the regressions (these other independent variables are changes in domestic spending on domestically produced goods and changes in labor requirements per unit of output) that are captured in the regression equation's constant term account for most of the deunionization. An anti-union shift in attitudes by most employers and workers across the economy, together with unfavorable new legislation and the hostile administration by government of existing labor laws—factors cited by labor unions and many labor economists as the main reason for deunionization—would be the type of "other factors" picked up by the constant term.

Trade has played a role in the deunionization process among basically educated union workers [workers with 12 or fewer years of education], in manufacturing, however. For the 1977–87 decade, for example, I estimate the disproportionately adverse (in terms of the relative importance of these two groups in the labor force) employment impact of increases in imports of manufactured goods on basically educated union compared with basically educated nonunion workers to be equal to about one-quarter of the negative impact on union membership that is measured by the constant term in the regression equation. In the 1987–97 decade, the employment-displacement pressures of increased imports were actually disproportionately lower on basically educated union workers than on basically educated nonunion workers.

However, increases in exports in the manufacturing sector during the 1987–97 period were unexpectedly associated with decreases (rather than increases) in the employment of basically educated union workers. I suggest that this effect, which almost offsets the favorable manner in which basically educated union workers fared on the import side, may be due to the positive correlation of export increases with such other factors as increases in foreign direct investment and foreign outsourcing. The main conclusion, however, is that factors other than industry changes in international trade or the other independent variables in the regression equation account for most of the decline in unionization in both periods.

"The modest revival of grassroots activity in the U.S. labor movement . . . has been largely missed by the mainstream press."

Labor Unions Are Making a Comeback

Chris Kutalik

The U.S. labor movement is down but not out, labor activist and journalist Chris Kutalik maintains in this viewpoint. Kutalik points to a range of recent developments that suggest union revitalization: an increase in the number of labor strikes in the airline and transit industries, internal reform in the automobile and longshore unions, increased union activism among immigrant workers in farm and port occupations, and the formation of new rank-and-file cross-union groups emphasizing solidarity and common goals. Kutalik calls these positive signs that organized labor can counter the corporate and government "assault on workers' living and working conditions." Chris Kutalik is coeditor of the cross-union national newsletter Labor Notes *in Detroit and a former local transit union officer in Austin, Texas.*

Chris Kutalik, "Is Labor Finally Showing Signs of a Comeback?" *CounterPunch*, April 20, 2006, www.counterpunch.org/kutalik04202006.html. Reproduced by permission.

As you read, consider the following questions:

1. What prompted the upsurge in union strikes in 2005, according to Kutalik?

2. How are dissidents in the United Auto Workers and International Longshoremen's Association reforming their unions from within, according to the author?

3. What positive effects have labor unions had in Gulf Coast reconstruction following Hurricane Katrina and opposition to the war in Iraq, in Kutalik's view?

A s labor activists from around the country and world con-verge[d] on Dearborn, Michigan in early May 2006 for the Labor Notes Conference, it's worth reflecting [on] hopes for a revitalization of the labor movement. . . .

The modest revival of grassroots activity in the U.S. labor movement at the end of 2005 has largely been missed by the mainstream press.

Strikes Up

According to the Bureau of National Affairs [BNA], there were 271 work stoppages in the first three quarters of 2005 as com-pared to 227 in all of 2004. And the BNA's numbers do not include many of the high-profile strikes at the end of 2005 which involved roughly 70,000 workers: Northwest Airlines mechanics and cleaners, Boeing aircraft manufacturing work-ers, California hospital workers, Philadelphia and New York City transit.

What's prompting all this activity? Emboldened by four years on the attack since 9/11, many employers used aggres-sive bargaining tactics in unprecedented ways in 2005. Pro-posed wage and health care cuts were far deeper than in pre-vious years—in some cases, unions were faced with the near-to-total loss of retiree health care, pensions, and at times the near-destruction of the unionized jobs themselves.

Union Members Are Becoming More Professional

"In 2007, the typical union member is more likely to be Hispanic or Asian-American, a bit older, and more likely to reside in the South," he said. "All of these reflect more general changes in our country. The most dramatic change, however, is that the typical 2007 union member is considerably more likely to be a female, a professional or manager, or a public-sector worker, and far less likely to work in manufacturing. These days, 'Joe Lunch Bucket' is increasingly likely to be 'Chris Briefcase.'"

Jack Fiorito, quoted in Barry Ray, "The State of Organized Labor,"
FSU News, Florida State University, January 16, 2007.

Caught off-guard by employers' intransigence at the table, a number of unions found themselves in last-minute "desperation strikes": badly prepared, yet seen as necessary for survival of the union.

Even if these strikes didn't produce the contractual gains that workers wanted, they did have some positive effects. Striking workers at Boeing and New York transit strikers, for instance, described seeing new excitement and participation from fellow workers following their successful, high-profile attempts to shut down their employers.

Many activists involved in strike support for the Northwest Airlines mechanics' strike saw striking mechanics and cleaners move month by month into greater militancy and awareness of the broader labor movement. Indeed, rank-and-file strikers from AMFA [Aircraft Mechanics Fraternal Association] Local 5 in Detroit formed their own Solidarity Committee that attended other unions' pickets, Jobs with Justice events, and various social movement events in the Detroit area.

Surge in Reform

Strikes were only one example of increased activity. Auto part manufacturer Delphi's announcement of bankruptcy—and plan for 63 percent wage cuts and massive layoffs—unleashed a wave of rank-and-file organizing.

While the UAW [United Auto Workers] leadership remained paralyzed, unable or unwilling to mount even a desperation fight, UAW members launched a new dissident organization: Soldiers of Solidarity (SOS). SOS successfully organized a highly publicized picket of several hundreds at the Detroit Auto Show, another large picket at Delphi's headquarters, and has been organizing trainings for UAW members in how to use work-to-rule strategies to fight the company inside the plants.

Outside of auto, reformers in the East Coast longshore union, the International Longshoreman's Association, continue to build the dissident Longshore Workers Coalition. In January 2006, transit workers in New York followed up their three-day strike by voting down the concessionary contract pushed by union leaders.

In Los Angeles, reform-minded teachers swept elections in the second-largest teacher union in the country, United Teachers of Los Angeles.

Rank-and-file work has also seen an uptick in the Teamsters as that union heads towards its 2006 elections. Teamster reformers have mounted the Strong Contracts/Good Pensions slate with Tom Leedham as their candidate for General President.

The 2006 campaign began with reform victories in local elections in Atlanta, Milwaukee, Louisville, and elsewhere. The grassroots campaign gathered over 50,000 member signatures in two months and received election accreditation in December.

Immigrant Worker Victories

Some of the biggest labor success stories of 2005 were made by predominantly immigrant farm workers. The Coalition of Immokalee Workers' successful Taco Bell boycott and the Farm Labor Organizing Committee's 5,000-worker organizing victory in North Carolina broke new ground for immigrant labor organizing.

Both groups won by organizing in the fields and communities at the same time—building successful national campaigns that mobilized faith-based, student, and other community-labor groups, while maintaining internal member-driven education.

On the waterfront, wildcat strikes at ports and inter-modal yards over the last two years have won victories on both coasts for mostly immigrant workers. Wildcat strikes at the Stockton, California, inter-modal yard in the spring and summer of 2005 were organized from a Sikh temple, for example.

The massive immigrant marches that sprang up around the United States in early 2006 give further evidence of a growing, vibrant immigrant rights movement. On April 10—the second round of protests—an estimated two million or more people marched in 140 cities.

Industrial Unity

2005 also saw the emergence of new rank-and-file groups advocating an old vision: industrial unity. These cross-union formations have evolved in the strategically important transportation industry, where union members face myriad challenges.

The Teamsters' absorption of two major rail craft unions (the Brotherhood of Locomotive Engineers and the Brotherhood of Maintenance of Way Employees) has sparked interesting organizing among rank-and-file activists in the rail industry. Frustrated by a century of craft division and feuding, union members began reaching out to other members across the craft and union divide last year by forming Rail Operating Crafts United.

In the embattled airline industry, union members and supporting activists have built a new cross-union, cross-craft group: Airline Workers United. AWU emerged in response to ongoing problems made clear by the Northwest Airlines strike—the collapse of solidarity, the unresponsiveness of many airline union leaderships, and the lack of an industry-wide union strategy.

AWU is currently made up of flight attendants, mechanics, gate workers, and customer service agents from a number of airline unions at Northwest, but it has also begun spreading to pilots and mechanics at United and American.

Social Movement Unionism

Beyond traditional union reform, labor groups fought for democracy and social justice in new and exciting ways in 2005 (labor's participation in the above-mentioned immigrant marches is one example of this).

Unions and other labor organizations continue to oppose the war in Iraq, with U.S. Labor Against the War (USLAW) playing the biggest role. USLAW is reaching out to veterans and military families, sponsoring public events with Military Families Speak Out, Iraqi Veterans Against the War, and other veterans groups.

In 2005, USLAW also organized a successful tour of Iraqi labor leaders and an intervention at the AFL-CIO Convention. Due to pressure from USLAW, the AFL-CIO passed a resolution against the war in Iraq at its convention, a groundbreaking moment for the federation.

Responding to the disaster of Hurricane Katrina, Community Labor United (CLU)—a Jobs with Justice-like community-labor coalition in New Orleans—stepped up its own regional organizing. CLU has already been involved in a number of local fights around Gulf Coast reconstruction, and continues to demand that the people of New Orleans determine the future of their city.

For all these positive developments, this remains a difficult period for U.S. labor. Union membership has hit historic lows, and employers (along with the government) continue their assault on workers' living and working conditions.

But precisely because this period looks so bleak, it is important to examine these victories, small and large, and learn what we can. In hard times we need the lessons these victories provide, and we also need inspiration.

> "Corruption in American unions isn't a
> matter of isolated felonious acts by
> individuals. . . . Some fraction of the
> membership is involved just as much as
> the leadership."

Labor Unions Are Corrupt and Exploit Workers

Robert Fitch

Labor journalist Robert Fitch is a lifelong union member and former union consultant in New York City. In this viewpoint, Fitch blames systemic corruption for the stagnation and decline of American labor unions over the past fifty years. Corrupt union officials and members jointly exploit union resources and power, according to Fitch, and honest union officials risk career suicide if they criticize the status quo. Fitch maintains that, with good reason, working people no longer trust unions and will not make sacrifices to support them, and the result is shrinking membership, failed organizing efforts, minimal strike activity, and union sweatshops whose conditions and wages are no better than those at nonunion sweatshops.

Robert Fitch, *Solidarity for Sale: How Corruption Destroyed the Labor Movement and Undermined America's Promise*. Cambridge, MA: Perseus Group, 2006, pp. 6–34. Copyright © 2006 by Robert Fitch. Reprinted by permission of Perseus Books, L.L.C.

As you read, consider the following questions:

1. According to Fitch's definition of corruption as "the private use of public office," what legal practices are just as corrupt as illegal practices and involve union members as well as union officials?

2. Why is it actually not in unions' interest to spend money on organizing campaigns, in the author's view?

3. Why are union pension plans underfunded and unable to meet their obligations, according to Fitch?

Corruption is properly understood as the private use of public office. When union corruption appears in the press, it's usually because of illegal acts, such as the outright pilfering of union assets or collusion with the boss selling the members' jobs or giving away their benefits. But a lot of corruption is legal—hiring your relatives, taking excessive salaries, hiring-hall favoritism.

Typically, pro-business conservatives stretch the definition of corruption too far by applying it to the actions of unions they don't like—militant strikes or violent political demonstrations, for example. Such actions may be illegal, and they may even be wrong, but they aren't corrupt: No one is exploiting the union for a private purpose.

While the political right seeks to widen the notion of corruption too far, the populist left would narrow it too much. For some leftist critics, only the actions of union officials can count as corrupt. The members are eternal victims.

Exempting the membership entirely means that corruption can't ever be understood as what it patently is: systemic. Corruption in American unions isn't a matter of isolated felonious acts by individuals or permeation from outside by American culture. The U.S. labor movement relies on its own internal system for producing corruption. Some fraction of the membership is involved just as much as the leadership. That's why it has lasted so long.

Organized labor's governance resembles the ancient fiefdoms. Like feudalism, the union system is local, territorial, and based on ties of mutual dependence and protection. Those who produce the revenue—union dues and manorial rents alike—are tied to the territory. Just as serfs couldn't switch manors, workers stay in their locals unless they want to give up their jobs. Just as the serfs paid feudal dues for the right to work the land, workers pay union dues for the right to stay on the job.

Power in the system rests on reciprocal ties between leaders and favored or connected members. Together they are able jointly to exploit the union's job control power. The most favored get union office, and the less favored get staff jobs or positions as stewards and foremen. In Teamsters Local 282, Sammy "the Bull" Gravano's old local, "working teamster foreman" jobs pay six figures—and you don't have to bounce around in the cab of a truck all day long. Foreman jobs are tied to the fortunes of the leaders who give them out. A client turning on his boss, even if the boss is charged with a felony, means giving up a comfortable livelihood.

Together patrons and clients transform unionism into a special interest—a faction that thrives at the expense of the common good. At the hard core may be the officers who use loyalty to create immunity. Those who rely on the officers for jobs are loath to give them up. But the leaders' long reach into the pockets of the disfavored members could hardly exist without sinews that connect them to a substantial fraction of the membership. . . .

Corruption's Source

A major journalistic conceit is the importance of character. By probing the lifestyle, background, convictions, ethnicity, and gender of the actor, you understand the person. If you understand the person, you understand the behavior of his institution.

If character is so decisive, how come union problems all seem so much the same, year after year, no matter who runs the institution? Whatever the gender, race, or intellectual background of the leaders, corruption has been a constant. District Council 37, the 120,000-member New York affiliate of the American Federation of State County and Municipal Employees, is run by a seventy-eight-year-old black woman, Lillian Roberts, a former nurse's aide. Her critics accuse her of responsibility for kickbacks, election irregularities, nepotism, benefit fund scams, and poor contracts. In 1998, her predecessor, Stanley Hill, a black man, resigned in the face of similar charges. But many of the rackets uncovered at the time by prosecutors originated in the era of his predecessor, Victor Gotbaum, a Jewish man who'd been an intelligence officer and served on the Council on Foreign Relations. Regardless of temperament or background, the job requires a certain combination of iron and rubber—an iron hand and rubber principles. The occupant either has them to begin with or acquires them soon.

Academics generally don't do character analysis. They have bigger theoretical fish to fry: globalization, the shift of manufacturing to the third world, the rise of the information economy, the feminization of the workforce. These universal trends are supposed to explain our unions' problems. How come, then, American unions are so different from unions elsewhere? Except in officer salaries and total union financial assets, where we're far ahead, the U.S. labor movement comes in last or nearly last in just about every other important respect: the lowest density, the longest decline in membership, the least success in social welfare legislation, the fewest strikes—America hasn't had a real general strike since 1877.

The American labor movement is not only weaker than others, it's also a lot more corrupt. Of course, some corruption is probably inevitable. But the scale and scope of corruption and self-enrichment in "old Europe" remain relatively underdeveloped. In other advanced industrialized countries, you don't find insignificant local leaders earning over half a million a year. Nor do you find whole unions run by crime families—not even in Sicily or Calabria. To realize their dream of becoming union leaders, young thugs like James "Big Jim" Colosimo, the founder of the Chicago Laborers and the longest-serving crime boss in the city's history, had to migrate in 1895 from southern Italy. Only in America!

The fundamental actors in American labor are institutions—the unions themselves. It's the union institutions that act and have identity, that manage or succumb to trends, and that shape the character of their leaders. The real question is not "Who is [AFL-CIO president] John Sweeney?" but "What is the institutional character of a labor movement that turns out John Sweeneys generation after generation?" What needs scrutiny is less the adverse macroeconomic trends than why the AFL-CIO [America's largest federation of labor unions] has been so notably unable to handle them. American unions share the problems of unions everywhere, but they also have deeper, characteristic problems.

Call it the fiefdom syndrome—a kind of protection system based on exclusive jurisdictions, exclusive bargaining, and job control. Those who control the jobs become the bosses; those who want the jobs become their clients. Loyalty to the boss becomes the highest virtue. It's an ethic of dependence rather than solidarity, one that promotes the most wide-ranging corruption. Corruption in turn produces atomization, weakness, demoralization, and apathy, which in turn promote further corruption. Solidarity—united action on behalf of the common good—turns into a slogan that produces only crooked smiles.

It's this special character that explains why the American labor movement fares so poorly in the vital tasks unions are designed to perform: improving the material living standards of the majority of working people, ending the dependence of workers on the will of the employer, and reducing the blatant economic inequality that tends to develop between those who run corporations and those who work for them.

How Corruption Has Undermined the Unions

Defenders of the AFL-CIO status quo argue that friends of the labor movement should shut up about corruption. Exposés of labor bosses, they say, only aid corporate bosses. The unstated assumption is that corruption has no damaging consequences of its own. It's just the *perception* of corruption that's harmful.

But corruption is not cost free, and in many ways its consequences are more serious than ever. This is true even though the gross symptoms are less obvious. It's not like in the late 1920s or the early 1930s; we don't have gunfights on street corners, with the Capone and the Moran gangs blasting away at each other for control of the Teamsters, laundry, janitors, and bartenders unions. Nowadays in Chicago, the Outfit has no rivals, and their bullets are delivered in envelopes, meant to scare dissidents, not kill them. Maintaining a territory requires a lot less firepower than seizing it in the first place. But the slow strangulation of genuine labor union impulses and energies has had its effect. The devastating results of the curse—five generations of corruption—can be measured in . . . specific ways.

The Continuing Shrinkage in Membership Numbers

Most critics point to a decline in dues-paying membership as the Federation's biggest problem. It's not. If the AFL-CIO's 13 million members were active, participating members, if they were connected in action and in sympathy with non-dues-paying workers in a genuine labor movement, if current union leaders had any moral authority, American labor might still be a powerful force in the country.

Still, the numerical decline says something about the fortunes of the Federation. When the AFL-CIO was created fifty

Union Leader Fraud and Corruption

Embezzlement, false reports, violence, and more. . . . Most people don't know just how many crimes are committed every year through which union officials hurt their own members. The number of reputed and verified crimes is staggering. Nothing illustrates this more clearly than the hundreds of indictments of union officials for violations of the Labor Management and Reporting Disclosure Act. According to the Office of Labor-Management Standards (OLMS), those crimes include "embezzlement, filing false reports, keeping false records, destruction of records, extortionate picketing and deprivation of rights by violence." The OLMS notes:

> In fiscal year 2005, OLMS completed 325 criminal cases. Indictments increased to 114, a 16 percent increase from FY 2001. The number of convictions dropped to 97. In addition, in FY 2005 court-ordered restitution amounted to $23,244,979.

That's $23 *million* in restitution ordered for victimizing union members and others.

UnionFacts.com,
"Union Leader Fraud & Corruption," 2006.

years ago, it had 16 million members, and private sector union density stood at nearly 40 percent. Now in the private sector, it's 8 percent. Public sector membership stands much higher, but it has stopped growing, and public sector workers constitute only about 15 percent of U.S. workers. Two Princeton labor economists predict that, given present trends, the entire U.S. labor movement—in the public and private sectors—will eventually bottom out at 2.1 percent.

Theories abound to explain the decline—including outsourcing, deindustrialization, globalization, the Reagan Revolution, bad labor laws, employer resistance, and the decline in the species of male, blue collar workers. But lacking is any recognition that stagnation is the natural state of official labor in America. From the dawn of the twentieth century, the periods of decline (1919–1934 and 1955–2004) are greater than the periods of growth (1900–1919 and 1934–1955).

Historically, the American Federation of Labor has tended toward stagnation for a lot of the same reasons corporate monopolies do. They are able to raise prices by restricting entry. They have little incentive to expand. Inefficiency, underinvestment, corruption, and inequality flow naturally from their restrictive efforts. . . .

The Failure to Organize

The total may represent only a third of the civilian-laborer force, but the AFL-CIO cites polls indicating that 15 million workers would like to join a union. Yet the AFL-CIO has only 13 million members. Neither Sweeney nor anyone in official labor was willing to admit that it simply wasn't in the interests of many unions to spend money on organizing. That's why they never did—and never will. . . .

In the classic trades—construction, longshore, and certain elite locals in the Teamsters, unions don't organize because bringing in more members wouldn't raise the income of those already organized. It would lower them. Many blacks, immigrants, and women would like to become plumbers and electricians, and many would like $100,000-a-year jobs on the docks. But from the union standpoint, bringing in these groups wouldn't increase the number of unionized jobs, just the number of workers sitting in the hiring hall waiting for jobs. There's also the danger that black members might dilute the political base of the white leadership.

Then there is the most unmentionable of internal organizing obstacles: corruption. Why didn't the Teamsters' Joint Council 25 boss, Bill Hogan, try to organize low-wage United Service Companies employees at the Las Vegas Convention Center? Why, in 1999, did he try to replace Las Vegas union workers making $20.00 an hour with employees from United making $7.90? Because his brother was a big executive in United, according to a Teamsters Internal Review Board, which expelled him for life. Why didn't Hogan's boss, [Jimmy] Hoffa Jr., set him straight? Most likely because gaining new members was less important to Hoffa than keeping the political support of his powerful regional baron.

Why don't union carpenters have a bigger share of the work in midtown Manhattan? Because the head of the New York City Council of Carpenters allegedly took an envelope with $10,000 inside. Prosecutors said it had been given to him by the son-in-law of the DeCavalcante crime family's godfather. The exchange took place after the two quaffed beers at Hooters, just a few steps from the Park Central Hotel. In exchange for the ten large—a down payment on a $50,000 bribe—Mike Forde, the Council's boss, agreed to allow lower-paid, non-union carpenters to replace his members on the Park Central remodeling job. Forde was convicted of the charges in 2004, but the conviction was later overturned by the presiding judge, Jeffrey Atlas, because of alleged anti-union sentiment on the part of some jurors. Atlas accused them of holding the view "that the case resembled a *Sopranos* episode." Perhaps the problem of juror bias could have been solved by excluding those contaminated with knowledge of the union's history. A decade earlier, Martin Forde, Mike's dad, was brought down on similar charges. The same charges doomed an almost unbroken series of District Council officials going back to the late Teddy Maritas, who allowed Genovese crime families to control a non-union drywall empire in the Bronx until he disappeared just before his trial.

The Decline in the Number
and Effectiveness of Strikes

Just consider the past fifty years. There was no great spike in strike activity in the 1950s—nothing like the strike wave following World War II, after price controls were lifted. But in 1952 there were 470 major strikes involving 2.75 million workers. The totals have dropped pretty steadily since. There was a flare-up in the 1970s—inflation again. But the numbers in the Nixon-Ford era never reached those of the Truman-Eisenhower period. And by 1992, there were only thirty-five strikes involving 364,000 workers. The percentage of work time lost by strikes fell to an oceanic depth of 0.02 percent—*two hundredths* of 1 percent.

Although it hardly seems possible, strike activity has fallen substantially since then. The 1997 Teamsters strike against UPS—heralded as a "watershed" by the secretary of labor and "a major triumph and an omen of future success" by the *New York Times*—proved to be a false dawn. The two-week strike didn't even change the ratio of full-time to part-time workers at UPS, much less reverse the decline of the U.S. labor movement. The downward trend continued unabated. In 2004, there were only seventeen strikes affecting only 0.01 percent of precious work time. The strike rate in the United States is only a fraction of what it is in major western European countries. . . .

The Collapse of Labor Standards

America Needs a Raise was the title of John Sweeney's book. His premise was that by putting resources into organizing unions, Americans could get a raise. But increasingly, many American unions weren't capable of getting raises that exceeded the non-union rate or sometimes even the minimum wage. Union wages below or only slightly higher than the legal minimums were common in the grocery stores and chicken-plucking factories represented by the UFCW, in factories and warehouses represented by the Teamsters, and, above all, in the restaurants and garment shops represented by UNITE-HERE.

For the immigrant workers represented by UNITE, attaining even the minimum wage was their American Dream. In 1997, a Bureau of Labor Standards report revealed that New York City, where UNITE had its headquarters, had the worst sweatshop problem in the nation. About two-thirds of the garment shops in the city were sweatshops, in violation of wage and hour or safety standards. The stunning finding, though, was that three-quarters of the *union* shops were sweatshops. The results seemed to conflict with the common wisdom that "a bad union is better than no union."

In fairness to union-run sweatshops, the government study didn't take into account that UNITE members had health and pensions benefits and non-union workers didn't. Still, the level of union benefits was extraordinarily low: a typical pensioner was receiving only $60–$70 a month—and that after a lifetime of body-destroying work, breathing air filled with cotton particles, bent over machines that required repetitive motion, often seven days a week, twelve hours a day. . . .

The Crisis of the $350 Billion Multiemployer Pension System

America's labor leaders manage a huge sum: over $350 billion in pension funds. Unfortunately, though, this sum is not nearly enough. Obligations exceed assets by at least $150 billion. Officials explain that the market's been down, and they talk about actuarial problems. But simple corruption and the fragmented character of the unions perhaps explain a great deal too.

One reason why there's not enough money to pay future obligations is that there are too many plans. Why does the AFL-CIO need to have 2,100 separate pension plans for its 13 million members? That's a plan for every 6,200 members. Social Security has one plan for all 280 million Americans. Social Security's administrative costs run about $11 a year per person. Take a Teamsters pension plan at random—Long Island City's Local 814. Administrative costs run about $420 each per year for the 2,700 member participants, who mostly work for moving companies. That's nearly forty times more per capita than what the Social Security Administration charges. The Bush administration insists that the sky is falling for Social Security because it will be able to meet only 70 percent of its obligations in 2040. *Today*, the Local 814 plan has only 55 percent of the funds it needs to meet its obligations.

It might well be that decades of control over Local 814 by the Bonanno crime family has shrunk the assets it needs. Still, a simple reduction in the number of union plans could save members billions in administrative costs—costs that consume a substantial portion of the plans' investment gain, and sometimes all of it. But consolidating the plans would mean less patronage and less power for the local union leaders who get to name trustees and hire outside vendors—and less opportunity for racketeering conspiracies.

Labor racketeers love pension funds. In 2002, a report by the Department of Labor's Office of the Inspector General showed that there were 357 pending racketeering investigations; 39 percent involved organized crime, and 44 percent involved pension or welfare plans.

It's often pension plan looting—not just adverse macroeconomic trends like low interest rates—that helps explain why union-run plans are so dangerously underfunded. The Teamsters' Central States Plan, "the Mob's piggy bank" during the 1970s and 1980s, can't pay its obligations today. UPS, the largest employer of Teamsters, touts *its* pension plans as fully funded. One of the saddest facts about the American labor movement is that the putative beneficiaries of union-run plans have been historically less likely to get a pension than workers who are beneficiaries of company-run plans.

> "Unions have set norms and established practices that become more generalized throughout the economy, thereby improving pay and working conditions for the entire workforce."

Labor Unions Benefit All Workers

Lawrence Mishel and Matthew Walters

In this viewpoint, economists Lawrence Mishel and Matthew Walters present evidence that labor unions not only increase union workers' pay and benefits, but set pay and benefit standards that nonunion employers follow. Mishel and Walters argue that unions also have played a major role in an array of labor laws and regulations that benefit all workers, including overtime pay, minimum wage, unemployment insurance, and worker's compensation. Lawrence Mishel is president of the Economic Policy Institute (EPI), a nonprofit, nonpartisan think tank in Washington, D.C., and principal author of the biannual research report The State of Working America. *Matthew Walters is an EPI research associate.*

As you read, consider the following questions:

1. How do labor unions lessen wage inequality, according to Mishel and Walters?
2. How do all workers benefit from what the authors call the "union threat effect"?
3. What workplace protections do the authors credit labor unions with providing for the U.S. workforce in general?

Unions have a substantial impact on the compensation and work lives of both unionized and non-unionized workers. . . .

Unions raise wages of unionized workers by roughly 20% and raise compensation, including both wages and benefits, by about 28%.

Unions reduce wage inequality because they raise wages more for low- and middle-wage workers than for higher-wage workers, more for blue-collar than for white-collar workers, and more for workers who do not have a college degree.

Strong unions set a pay standard that nonunion employers follow. For example, a high school graduate whose workplace is not unionized but whose industry is 25% unionized is paid 5% more than similar workers in less unionized industries.

The impact of unions on total nonunion wages is almost as large as the impact on total union wages.

The most sweeping advantage for unionized workers is in fringe benefits. Unionized workers are more likely than their nonunionized counterparts to receive paid leave, are approximately 18% to 28% more likely to have employer-provided health insurance, and are 23% to 54% more likely to be in employer-provided pension plans.

Unionized workers receive more generous health benefits than nonunionized workers. They also pay 18% lower health care deductibles and a smaller share of the costs for family coverage. In retirement, unionized workers are 24% more likely to be covered by health insurance paid for by their employer.

Unionized workers receive better pension plans. Not only are they more likely to have a guaranteed benefit in retirement, their employers contribute 28% more toward pensions.

Unionized workers receive 26% more vacation time and 14% more total paid leave (vacations and holidays).

Unions play a pivotal role both in securing legislated labor protections and rights such as safety and health, overtime, and family/medical leave and in enforcing those rights on the job. Because unionized workers are more informed, they are more likely to benefit from social insurance programs such as unemployment insurance and workers compensation. Unions are thus an intermediary institution that provides a necessary complement to legislated benefits and protections.

The Union Wage Premium

It should come as no surprise that unions raise wages, since this has always been one of the main goals of unions and a major reason that workers seek collective bargaining. How much unions raise wages, for whom, and the consequences of unionization for workers, firms, and the economy have been studied by economists and other researchers for over a century (for example, the work of Alfred Marshall). This section presents evidence from the 1990s that unions raise the wages of unionized workers by roughly 20% and raise total compensation by about 28%. . . .

The data most frequently used for this analysis is the Current Population Survey (CPS) of the Bureau of Labor Statistics, which is most familiar as the household survey used to report the unemployment rate each month. The CPS reports the wages and demographic characteristics (age, gender, education, race, marital status) of workers, including whether workers are union members or covered by a collective bargaining contract, and employment information (e.g., industry, occupation). Using these data, [Barry T.] Hirsch and [David A.] Macpherson (2003) found a union wage premium of 17.8% in 1997. Using data from a different, but also commonly used, household survey—the Census Bureau's Survey of Income and Program Participation (SIPP)—[Bethney] Gundersen (2003) found a union premium of 24.5%. So, estimates from household surveys that allow for detailed controls of worker characteristics find a union wage premium ranging from 15% to 25% in the 1990s. . . .

Historically, unions have raised the wages to a greater degree for "low-skilled" than for "high-skilled" workers. Consequently, unions lessen wage inequality. Hirsch and [Edward J.] Schumacher (1998) consider the conclusion that unions boost wages more for low- and middle-wage workers, a "universal finding" of the extensive literature on unions, wages, and worker skills. As they state:

> The standard explanation for this result is that unions standardize wages by decreasing differentials across and within job positions so that low-skilled workers receive a larger premium relative to their alternative nonunion wage. . . .

Unions and Fringe Benefits

In an earlier era, non-wage compensation was referred to as "fringe benefits." However, items such as adequate health insurance, a secure retirement pension, and sufficient and flexible paid leave to manage work and family life are no longer considered "fringe" components of pay packages. Thus, the union impact on benefits is even more critical to the lives of workers now than in the past. This section presents evidence that unionized workers are given employer-provided health and pension benefits far more frequently than comparable nonunion workers. Moreover, unionized workers are provided better paid leave and better health and pension plans. . . .

Union workers' paid leave benefits are 11.4% higher in dollar terms, largely because of the higher value of the benefits provided (8.0% of the total 11.4% impact). Unions have a far larger impact on pensions and health insurance, raising the value of these benefits by 56% and 77.4%, respectively. For pensions, the higher value reflects both that unionized workers are more likely to receive this benefit in the first place and that the pension plan they receive is generally a "richer" one. For health benefits, the value added by unions mostly comes from the fact that union workers receive a far more generous health plan than nonunionized workers. This factor accounts for 52.7% of the total 77.4% greater value that organized workers receive. . . .

Union workers also get more paid time off. This includes having 26.6% more vacation (or 0.63 weeks—three days) than nonunion workers. Another estimate, which includes vacations and holidays, indicates that union workers enjoy 14.3% more paid time off.

Union Wages, Nonunion Wages, and Total Wages

There are several ways that unionization's impact on wages goes beyond the workers covered by collective bargaining to affect nonunion wages and labor practices. For example, in industries and occupations where a strong core of workplaces are unionized, nonunion employers will frequently meet union standards or, at least, improve their compensation and labor practices beyond what they would have provided if there were no union presence. This dynamic is sometimes called the "union threat effect," the degree to which nonunion workers get paid more because their employers are trying to forestall unionization.

There is a more general mechanism (without any specific "threat") in which unions have affected nonunion pay and practices: unions have set norms and established practices that

Unions Help Bring Low-Wage Workers Out of Poverty

Average Hourly Earnings of Union and Nonunion Workers in Selected Occupations, 2006

	Union		Nonunion
	Hourly Wage ($)	Amount Above Poverty Line ($)	Hourly Wage ($)
Cashiers	$11.87	$ 4,075	$8.11
Child Care Workers	$10.84	$ 1,932	$8.59
Cleaners of Vehicles and Equipment	$13.34	$ 7,132	$8.87
Combined Food Preparation and Serving Workers, Including Fast Food	$10.09	$ 372	$8.00
Cooks	$12.45	$ 5,281	$8.61
Dining Room and Cafeteria Attendants and Bartender Helpers	$10.43	$ 1,079	$8.02
Food Preparation Workers	$11.95	$ 4,241	$7.98
Food Servers, Nonrestaruant	$13.45	$ 7,361	$9.39
Library Assisstants, Clerical	$13.94	$ 8,380	$9.76
Maids and Housekeeping Cleaners	$11.91	$ 4,158	$9.06
Other Protective Service Workers, Including Life Guards	$14.73	$10,023	$9.65
Packers and Packagers, Hand	$11.62	$ 3,555	$9.36
Personal and Home Care Aides	$10.38	$ 975	$9.15
Refuse and Recyclable Material Collectors	$21.50	$24,105	$9.12
Waiters and Waitresses	$14.30	$ 9,129	$9.81

*To surpass the poverty level for a family of four, a worker needs to earn an hourly wage of at least $9.92 (full-time, year round). The poverty line in 2006 for a family of four was $20,615.

TAKEN FROM: Barry T. Hirsch and David A. MacPherson, *Union Membership and Earnings Data Book*, BNA, 2007, forthcoming, U.S. Census Bureau, Preliminary Estimates of Weighted Average Poverty Thresholds for 2006, Jan. 24, 2007. Prepared by the AFL-CIO.

become more generalized throughout the economy, thereby improving pay and working conditions for the entire work-force. This has been especially true for the 75% of workers who are not college educated. Many "fringe" benefits, such as pensions and health insurance, were first provided in the union sector and then became more generalized—though . . . not universal. Union grievance procedures, which provide "due process" in the workplace, have been mimicked in many nonunion workplaces. Union wage-setting, which has gained exposure through media coverage, has frequently established standards of what workers generally, including many non-union workers, expect from their employers. Until the mid-1980s, in fact, many sectors of the economy followed the "pattern" set in collective bargaining agreements. As unions weakened, especially in the manufacturing sector, their ability to set broader patterns has diminished. However, unions remain a source of innovation in work practices (e.g., training, worker participation) and in benefits (e.g., child care, work-time flexibility, sick leave). . . .

Unions and Workplace Protections

An extensive array of labor laws and regulations protects workers in the labor market and the workplace. From the National Labor Relations Act and Social Security Act of 1935 to the Occupational Safety and Health Act of 1970 and the Family Medical Leave Act of 1993, labor unions have been instrumental in securing labor legislation and standards. However, beyond their role in initiating and advocating enactment of these laws and regulations, unions have also played an important role in enforcing workplace regulations. Unions have provided labor protections for their members in three important ways: 1) they have been a voice for workers in identifying where laws and regulations are needed, and have been influential in getting these laws enacted; 2) they have provided information to members about workers' rights and available programs; and 3) they have encouraged their members to exercise workplace rights and participate in programs by reducing fear of employer retribution, helping members navigate the necessary procedures, and facilitating the handling of workers' rights disputes.

Unions have played a prominent role in the enactment of a broad range of labor laws and regulations covering areas as diverse as overtime pay, minimum wage, the treatment of immigrant workers, health and retirement coverage, civil rights, unemployment insurance and workers' compensation, and leave for care of newborns and sick family members. Common to all of these rules is a desire to provide protections for workers either by regulating the behavior of employers or by giving workers access to certain benefits in times of need. Over the years, these rules have become mainstays of the American workplace experience, constituting expressions of cherished public values.

Less well recognized perhaps, is the important role that unions play in ensuring that labor protections are not just "paper promises" at the workplace. Government agencies charged with the enforcement of regulations cannot monitor every workplace nor automate the issuance of insurance claims resulting from unemployment or injury. In practice, the effectiveness of the implementation of labor protections depends on the worker's decision to act. This is done either by reporting an abuse or filing a claim. Unions have been crucial in this aspect by giving workers the relevant information about their rights and the necessary procedures, but also by facilitating action by limiting employer reprisals, correcting disinformation, aggregating multiple claims, providing resources to make a claim, and negotiating solutions to disputes on behalf of workers.

Evidence of the vital role of unions in implementing labor protections can be found in the research on various programs and benefits. Union membership significantly increases the likelihood that a worker will file a claim or report an abuse. Examples of this research can be found in such areas as unemployment insurance, worker's compensation, the Occupational Safety and Health Act, the Family Medical Leave Act, pensions, and the Fair Labor Standards Act's overtime provision. . . .

The research evidence clearly shows that the labor protections enjoyed by the entire U.S. workforce can be attributed in large part to unions. The workplace laws and regulations, which unions helped to pass, constitute the majority of the labor and industrial relations policies of the United States. However, these laws in and of themselves are insufficient to change employer behavior and/or to regulate labor practices and policies. Research has shown convincingly that unions have played a significant role in enforcing these laws and ensuring that workers are protected and have access to benefits to which they are legally entitled. Unions make a substantial and measurable difference in the implementation of labor laws.

Legislated labor protections are sometimes considered alternatives to collective bargaining in the workplace, but the fact of the matter is that a top-down strategy of legislating protections may not be influential unless there is also an effective voice and intermediary for workers at the workplace—unions. In all of the research surveyed, no institutional factor appears as capable as unions of acting in workers' interests. Labor legislation and unionization are best thought of as complements, not substitutes. . . .

Unions enable due process in the workplace and facilitate a strong worker voice in the broader community and in politics. Many observers have stated, correctly, that a strong labor movement is essential to a thriving democracy.

Periodical Bibliography

The following articles have been selected to supplement the diverse views presented in this chapter.

Dale Belman and Paula B. Voos	"Union Wages and Union Decline: Evidence from the Construction Industry," *Industrial and Labor Relations Review*, October 2006.
Bureau of Labor Statistics	"Union Members in 2006," *U.S. Department of Labor News*, January 25, 2007.
Human Events.com	"Top 10 Labor Union Power Grabs," March 13, 2007.
Charlene M. Kalenkoski and Donald J. Lacombe	"Right-to-Work Laws and Manufacturing Employment," *Southern Economic Journal*, vol. 73, no. 2, October 2006.
Kris Maher and Janet Adamy	"Do Hot Coffee and 'Wobblies' Go Together?" *Wall Street Journal*, March 21, 2006.
Lawrence Mishel	"The Right to Organize, Freedom, and the Middle-Class Squeeze," *Viewpoints, Economic Policy Institute*, March 27, 2007.
Multinational Monitor	"Undermining Democracy: Worker Repression in the United States," interview of David Bonior, vol. 27, no. 4, July—August 2006.
Nathan Newman	"The Brilliance of Labor," *Labor Blog*, September 3, 2006.
National Right to Work Committee	"The Problem of Compulsory Unionism," 2007. www.right-to-work.org/about/the problem.php.
NOW	"Meatpacking in the U.S.: Still a 'Jungle' Out There?" PBS, December 15, 2006. www.pbs.org.now/shows/250/meat-pack ing.html.
Charles J. Whalen	"Echoes of a Broken Strike," *Washington Post*, August 5, 2006.

OPPOSING
VIEWPOINTS®
SERIES

CHAPTER 2

How Have Immigration and Globalization Affected Labor Unions?

Chapter Preface

In 1924, union leader Samuel Gompers, founder of the American Federation of Labor (AFL), urged Congress to pass a restrictive anti-immigration act. Gompers warned legislators that the pro-immigration movement was backed by two "hostile forces of considerable strength":

> One of these is composed of corporation employers who desire to employ physical strength (broad backs) at the lowest possible wage and who prefer a rapidly revolving labor supply at low wages to a regular supply of American wage earners at fair wages. The other is composed of racial groups in the United States who oppose all restrictive legislation because they want the doors left open for an influx of their countrymen regardless of the menace to the people of their adopted country.

Congress enacted the protectionist legislation Gompers wanted. For more than thirty years, annual immigration averaged 200,000 or less per year and labor unions reached their highest levels of power and size, representing 30 percent of American workers.

In 1965, the federal government enacted immigration reforms that opened the door to millions of immigrants from Asia and from Mexico and other Latin American countries. American labor unions continued to oppose mass legal immigration, guest-worker proposals, and amnesty measures for the growing population of illegal immigrants, which by 2000 was estimated at 7 million and increasing by a half-million per year.

The era of mass immigration that began in 1965 coincided with a steady decline in union membership that continues to the present day. Many union supporters blame largely poor and less educated immigrants. In their view, Gompers's fears have been realized; a flood of immigrants means an oversupply of labor, and large numbers of nonunion workers who will do the work for less money under worse conditions inevitably means union jobs are lost, wages are depressed, and strikes are no longer effective against unfair employer practices.

But others reject this cause-and-effect relationship. They blame other federal policies (such as free trade agreements that allowed the importation of cheaper products produced by nonunion labor outside the United States), corporate greed (for shifting manufacturing overseas or squeezing employees to raise profits), the baby boom (which entered the labor market just as immigration controls were relaxed), or unions' own history of corruption and internal squabbling for union decline.

The hard reality is that unions are increasingly desperate for new members, and immigrants represent a huge potential pool of recruits (as well as a significant political constituency—politicians need immigrant support and unions need politicians' support). In 2001, amid bitter internal debate and public anti-immigration sentiment, the AFL-CIO broke from the past. According to Cornell University labor relations expert Vernon Briggs, the union federation announced its support for

> expanded immigration, lenient enforcement of immigration laws, and the legislative agenda of immigrants (which include repeal of sanctions against employers who hire illegal immigrants, generous amnesties for . . . illegal immigrants already in the United States . . . and liberalizing restrictions on foreign guest workers who seek to work in the United States).

This platform exacerbated internal dissent in the union, which culminated in the AFL-CIO and Change to Win split in 2005. The viewpoints in chapter 2 examine the relevance and viability of labor unions in today's increasingly global economy and debate the question of whether organized labor can be simultaneously for the American worker and for immigration.

> "With only 12 percent of U.S. workers in unions, we can't afford to limit our numbers. We need to draw our strength from unity with migrant labor."

Labor Unions and Immigrant Workers Must Support Each Other

CLR Working Group on Immigration

U.S. labor unions have historically opposed mass immigration, fearing that poor immigrants would accept substandard wages and working conditions, jeopardizing native-born workers' jobs and unions' bargaining power. In 2000, however, the AFL-CIO changed its position and advocated legalization and full labor rights for undocumented immigrants. In this viewpoint, the Center for Labor Renewal (CLR) applauds this step and argues the fundamental principle that all workers are legitimate, regardless of immigration status, and deserve full rights to unionize and a clear path to citizenship. Only by banding together in global unions with cross-border solidarity, the CLR insists, can workers reverse union decline and force corporations and governments to raise wages, improve conditions, and protect jobs in the global workplace. The Center for Labor Renewal, formed in 2006, is a

CLR Working Group on Immigration, "CLR Statement on Worker Migration," *www.centerforlaborrenewal.org*, April 24, 2007. Reproduced by permission.

pro-immigrant group of union members, workers, and educators dedicated to working-class organizing and activism.

As you read, consider the following questions:

1. According to the Center for Labor Renewal, how have multinational corporations forced displaced workers to cross national borders to work for substandard wages and conditions?
2. Why do the authors support immigration and immigrant unionization but oppose congressional guest-worker proposals?
3. In the authors' view, how do employers use the *Hoffman Plastics* ruling to keep undocumented immigrants from organizing unions?

Our nation is debating immigration in a climate of fear, mass workplace raids, and political backlash against the rising movement for immigrant rights. Many workers are responding to the rhetoric of division which blames disappearing job security and downward mobility on immigrants. Some unions are struggling against the odds to organize immigrants without working papers while others are simply giving up, saying it's impossible. . . .

Global Capital Has Created a Global Workforce

In the past 30 years, corporations have torn down national barriers and created a single world economy with a global labor market. Workers in one country now compete with others around the world. No worker is safe: factories are leaving Western Europe for Eastern Europe and Mexico for China.

In opening up the entire world for trade and investment, transnational corporations are displacing hundreds of millions of workers. One example among many is NAFTA, the US-Canada-Mexico free trade agreement. In 1994 NAFTA opened

Mexico to massive imports of US corn, driving an estimated two million people off their land. Looking for work, peasants flooded into Mexico's cities and factories along the US border. There they were joined by urban Mexican workers displaced by US companies including Wal-Mart, which took over or bankrupted Mexican companies. Many of these displaced workers kept traveling north and crossed the border, at least half a million a year. The money Mexican migrant laborers send home now subsidizes the low wages paid in Mexico by Delphi, General Electric, Hyundai, and Levi Strauss or their suppliers. Those "family remittances" outpace all sources of foreign income for Mexico, and the same is true for El Salvador, Palestine, the Philippines, and a growing number of countries. . . .

According to the United Nations, nearly 200 million people work outside their countries of birth, and an equal number are migrants inside their own countries. Global worker migration has provoked a global backlash. The backlash is led by nativists who fear a rising tide of brown-skinned workers. Their vision is symbolized by the wall on the US border with Mexico. They spar with a business lobby that seeks to keep cheap labor flowing, if not through undocumented workers then through vastly expanding guest worker programs.

Nativists blame immigrants for flat wages, scarce jobs, and our declining labor movement. However, the responsibility lies with corporations that launched an all-out assault on wages and unions in the 1970s—well before today's wave of migration began. Industries like meatpacking destroyed solid union jobs in the 1970s and replaced them with low-wage jobs in places far from the centers of union power. The [Ronald] Reagan and [George H. W.] Bush administrations busted unions and shifted the tax burden from corporations and wealth-holders to middle-class and working families. The IMF [International Monetary Fund] and World Bank reproduced this scenario around the world, driving down wages and worker

Unions Want to Bring Illegal Immigrants into Fold

Some of the nation's labor organizations are calling for legalization of all the nation's undocumented workers and have conceded the guest worker issue.

"There is no good reason why any immigrant who comes to this country prepared to work, to pay taxes, and to abide by our laws and rules should be denied what has been offered to immigrants throughout our country's history—a path to legal citizenship," said Ana Avendano, assistant general counsel for the AFL-CIO [American Federation of Labor and Congress of Industrial Organization], which represents 53 unions nationally.

The AFL-CIO and the Change to Win coalition, collectively representing about 15 million workers, or about 12.7 percent of the U.S. labor force, say undocumented workers need to be brought into the fold.

Devona Walker, "Unions Want to Bring Undocumented Workers into Fold," HeraldTribune.com, July 19, 2006.

rights in at least 90 countries, under IMF "structural adjustment programs." Immigrants aren't destroying the "blue collar middle class"; corporations are.

Now the corporate drive to cut labor costs is moving into the white-collar, professional middle class. High-tech firms are outsourcing work to lower-cost companies in India and China while they import skilled workers under H-1B and L1 visas. Job export and migrant worker import are two arcs of the same vicious circle.

On our next trip around that circle we'll encounter guest worker programs. Guest worker programs tie a worker to a particular job and employer. They are a key component of the World Bank's new development policy, which uses migrant workers' family remittances to keep their native countries from collapsing. Current trade negotiations in the WTO (World Trade Organization) would establish a global guest worker program through GATS, the General Agreement on Trade in Services. GATS lays out all the ways companies can find cheaper workers in the global labor market. GATS Mode 1, "move the work," means that healthcare companies (for example) get their x-rays read overseas. GATS Mode 2, "move the client," is reflected in 'medical tourism,' where patients go overseas for operations where the labor is cheaper. Mode 3 applies to investment abroad and GATS Mode 4, not yet adopted, would establish a guest worker program for the entire world. If it succeeds, virtually all workers in the US will be exposed to competition from guest workers who have been stripped of fundamental human rights.

Immigrant Workers and Unions Succeed or Fail Together

Today many workers and some unions think that penalizing employers will help solve the problem of global wage competition. However, workplace enforcement of immigration law is used to break up organizing drives, intimidate workers, and keep them from organizing. Employers are rarely prosecuted vigorously for hiring undocumented workers and almost never criminally charged for abusing them. On paper, immigrants with or without documentation have the same labor rights as all other U.S. workers, including the right to form unions. However, the 2002 *Hoffman Plastics* decision (ruling that employers don't have to pay back wages when they illegally fire undocumented workers organizing unions) took the enforcement teeth out of those laws.

Foreign-born workers don't send factories overseas, freeze wages, cut benefits, deskill jobs, or bust union organizing drives in this country. Corporations do. Attacks on immigrants will not save US workers from the labor movement's long decline. We're all part of the same labor force now. If we fight among ourselves, we will just make it easier for employers to pit us against one another. US labor history is filled with the wreckage of exclusionism. We must learn to advance our collective interests. . . .

We need worker-centered solutions that respect the following principles:

1. All workers are legitimate members of the workforce, regardless of their immigration status. All should have full labor rights, including the right to organize. Those rights must be fully enforced, and if they are, most of the immigration "problem" will disappear—at least from workers' point of view.

2. No human being is illegal. All people were born with inalienable human rights, and real immigration reform must decriminalize migrant workers. It must allow reunification for immediate families and establish a clear path to citizenship for those who wish to stay permanently.

3. Guest worker programs are inherently a contract labor program that is a form of servitude. The right to work should belong to the worker, not the boss. No real immigration reform can tie workers to particular employers or jobs.

4. People should be able to work and survive in their own countries. We need to build solidarity with workers, labor organizations and movements around the world, end IMF austerity programs, and replace them with true development. Trade and development policies should create internal markets and jobs that provide for the basic needs of the world's population.

The AFL-CIO took a huge step in 2000 when it supported legalization, full labor rights, and an end to employer sanctions. Now its member unions need to talk about that with their members. Some are still mired mentally in the 1950s, when trade unionists collaborated with imperial wars and corporate exploitation in the global South to gain a small slice of the pie for a shrinking portion of the U.S. workforce. Labor relied on exclusion, and exclusion is still much of our culture and practice. With only 12 percent of U.S. workers in unions, we can't afford to limit our numbers. We need to draw our strength from unity with migrant labor and solidarity with workers throughout the world.

These objectives require organizational work. Our top-down, no-room-for-debate, no-time-for-education culture resists change. Our movement must devote time and energy to educating bottom-up on immigration, globalization, and rebuilding a powerful workers' movement. CLR believes in a labor movement creative and open enough to unite U.S.-born and foreign-born workers with workers around the world. We need a debate that will lead to alliances with new organizations and welcome workers into a new labor movement.

Long-Term and Short-Term Strategies

There's no quick fix to the declining strength of labor. Therefore we call for long-range solutions while addressing urgent tasks and needs for foreign-born workers.

Capital has gone global. So must labor. Until it does, corporations will evade us where we are strong and whipsaw us where we are weak. If capital can open borders to trade and lower tariffs, so too must labor fight to have the right to cross borders—and organize unions that can force corporations and governments to respect full labor rights and raise regional and global wages. To accomplish this goal, we must build worker power by constructing egalitarian and democratic global unions and cross-border solidarity. The U.S. labor movement must oppose U.S. imperial power and support sister labor movements in the global South.

As for immediate demands and needs, many immigrants live in constant danger of job loss and deportation and have waited years to unite their families. We must support a clear, prompt path to citizenship and visas for family reunification. Unfortunately, citizenship is being offered as part of a package that also includes guest worker programs. We must push Congress to oppose expanded guest worker programs. If Congress enacts them as part of a compromise, we must continue working together—in our unions, worker centers, and immigrant rights organizations—to stop guest worker programs from driving down wages, worker rights and leverage. We must monitor conditions, protest the inevitable abuses, and lend support to guest worker union organizing. We must start now to build a movement to reduce and abolish this renewed form of servitude. . . .

Finally, we need to stress what all workers suffer in common: an absence of the right to organize to raise wages and improve conditions, inadequate education and opportunity, the loss of good jobs, the incarceration of millions of able-bodied youth in our prisons and their diversion into the military. Whether you're U.S. or foreign-born, whether you have documents or not, all workers share a common goal of dignity and respect and this should be the way we frame the issue.

> *"Huge influxes of immigrants, even if successfully organized, will wind up undercutting union collective-bargaining ability."*

Union Support of Immigration Is Self-Defeating

Carl F. Horowitz

Carl F. Horowitz is director of the Organized Labor Accountability Project of the National Legal and Policy Center, a nonprofit group promoting ethics in American public life, based in Falls Church, Virginia. In this viewpoint, Horowitz warns that organized labor's alliance with "ethnic radicals" and big business in supporting mass immigration is dangerously misguided. Horowitz claims that proposed guest-worker programs amount to amnesty—there is no way to ensure "temporary" workers will return home—and amnesty only encourages more illegal immigration, which polls show 63 percent of Americans consider a very serious problem. Furthermore, he argues, union leaders are not looking out for their members: They frankly admit they want to work with immigrants to boost union revenues and viability, even though 60 percent of union households object to amnesty proposals.

As you read, consider the following questions:

1. Both the AFL-CIO and Change to Win support immigrant organizing. How do the two union federations' positions on this issue differ, according to the author?

2. According to Horowitz, why do union leaders support a massive guest-worker program, siding with instead of fighting corporations on the immigration issue?

3. How would large numbers of new immigrant members actually hurt unions' collective bargaining ability, in Horowitz's opinion?

The AFL-CIO argues that labor must lobby Congress for legislation to adjust the legal status of immigrants living here illegally as a prerequisite to effective organizing. By contrast, [rival union federation] Change to Win asserts that organizing massive numbers of immigrants is necessary for lobbying. The two entities differ over cause and effect, not substance.

Indeed, if anything, Change to Win has *more* to gain through mass immigration. The federation's two fastest-growing unions, SEIU (1.8 million members) and the United Food and Commercial Workers (1.4 million members), represent large numbers of unskilled immigrant workers in labor-intensive industries. All those Third World newcomers working at Wal-Mart, Cintas, McDonald's and Wendy's overwhelmingly work for companies that CTW-member unions see as targets in corporate campaigns.

Change of Mind

Organized labor actually was a latecomer to support for mass immigration. Indeed, for more than a century unions were conspicuous by their resistance to it. Union leaders feared that desperate immigrants would accept wages, benefits and working conditions that native-born workers would find unacceptable. In large enough numbers, such immigrants could pose a threat to the unions' hope to achieving bargaining power, even if over the long run they might indirectly spur union membership. Such fears, in retrospect, have proven justified. "[E]very serious study over the past 100 years," notes Cornell University labor economist Vernon Briggs, "has found that wages are depressed by immigration, the adverse impact being most severe for unskilled workers." . . .

Self-interest had governed organized labor's earlier opposition to mass immigration: it also lay at the heart of labor's reversal. Illegal Mexican, Salvadoran, and Filipino workers no longer were viewed as competitors with native-born workers for scarce jobs. Now, the unions explained, they were the very future of organizing drives, a great untapped resource. Labor now was primed to join the alliance of employers and ethnic politicians of which [union founder] Samuel Gompers warned against decades earlier.

Pro-Immigration Triumvirate

The alliance between labor and business was logical, though rooted in opposite motives. Trade groups such as the National Association of Manufacturers, the U.S. Chamber of Commerce and the National Restaurant Association support normalizing the immigration status of illegal workers. Randel Johnson, the U.S. Chamber of Commerce vice president on labor and immigration issues, for example, reacted favorably when the [George W.] Bush administration unveiled its guest-worker plan in January 2004. "We need a system of 'earned targeted adjustment' for undocumented workers that fill vital roles in the economy, which would enable them to achieve legal status," he said. Union leaders, for their part, continue to rail against "the corporations" in their press releases and convention speeches, but they are full partners on immigration. And why should they not be? Few things are more potentially mutually advantageous than a massive guest-worker program—an amnesty all but in name—in which temporary immigrant workers pay into employer or union benefit funds but do not stay around long enough to collect.

By contrast, the alliance between unions and ethnic radicals owes more to political beliefs than economic interests. Each is an indispensable bloc within the Democratic Party. The ethnic advocacy groups—most of all, the Mexican American Legal Defense and Educational Fund (MALDEF)—are aggressive in filing lawsuits to promote immigration, while pressuring employers to commit themselves to ever-greater ethnic "diversity."

Labor organizations have come to see America in much the same terms as the allies in MALDEF, the National Council of La Raza and the League of United Latin American Citizens. They believe Hispanic and other Third World immigrants are America's victims who can be organized into a coalition of "people of color." In August 2003, for example, the AFL-CIO issued a statement, "In Support of Immigration Reform." Its dozens of signers included unions such as the Teamsters and the Operating Engineers, but also a farrago of nonprofits such as MALDEF, the Mexico Solidarity Network, the Hispanic Farmers Association of El Paso, the Tennessee Immigrant Rights Coalition and the National Immigration Project of the (far-Left) National Lawyers Guild. The statement supported "a fair and realistic process to provide an adjustment of status for undocumented workers" and opposed "the expansion of existing temporary non-immigrant worker programs or the creation of any such new programs at this time."

The labor-ethnic alliance is producing more than manifestos. In 2001 the AFL-CIO Executive Council, the General Amnesty Coalition and other groups co-sponsored a May Day March for Workers' Rights and March for Immigrant Rights. The Organizing Committee for Workers Rights held a May Day rally and concert in New York City's Union Square under

Industrial Unions and Service Unions Are Split over Immigration Reform

The AFL-CIO and large industrial unions [have] historically seen illegal immigrants as unwanted competitors to their membership. (However, in recent years, the AFL-CIO has made efforts to reach out to illegal immigrants, including an alliance in 2006 with a network representing day labors.)

The other side includes the Service Employees International Union, whose members have healthcare, property management and public service jobs, and Unite Here, which represents garment, hotel and restaurant workers. These unions have embraced immigrants, even those here illegally. . . .

Industrial union leaders oppose [immigration legislation] provisions that would create a temporary-worker program for 200,000 immigrants each year, a transient workforce they fear would erode wages and working conditions.

Service workers' unions are more willing to accept an amended version of the temporary-worker program because of provisions that would legalize an estimated 12 million people now here illegally. Industrial unions are skeptical of legalization.

Molly Hennessy-Fiske, *"Unions Split over Immigration Bill,"*
Los Angeles Times, *June 1, 2007.*

the slogan, "Amnesty for all immigrants—present and future." Later, in October 2003, [AFL-CIO president John] Sweeney welcomed illegal aliens to a pro-amnesty "freedom ride," a bus convoy that converged on Liberty State Park in New Jersey. As of this writing, the Massachusetts chapter of a labor-backed group, Jobs with Justice, is trying to persuade that state's legislature to pass a bill enabling "undocumented" (i.e., illegal) immigrant college students to pay in-state tuition, joining nine other states at present with such laws.

Unions' Quandary

Support for amnesty is the culmination of the immigration-without-consequences mentality. It lacks even the pretense of distinguishing legality from illegality. Of course, "amnesty" is a very unpopular word. That's precisely why President [George] Bush adamantly denies that his guest-worker program constitutes an amnesty. But underneath the lofty rhetoric is the reality that the proposal lacks effective enforcement mechanisms to ensure that those who obtain renewable "temporary" three-year visas will return home. The Government Accountability Office recently admitted in a draft report, in fact, that the agency overseeing the program, U.S. Citizenship and Immigration Services, would not have a fraud-management system in place until 2011. It looks like amnesty under a new name.

The Bush guest-worker plan, plus a number of similar proposals circulating in the Senate, fails to take into account that each announcement of amnesty encourages more of the same. There is never a "final" amnesty, merely a period of respite before the next one. That's why Harvard political scientist Samuel Huntington terms immigration a "self-perpetuating" process.

Labor leaders fear a loss of revenues, bargaining power and visibility that would come with curtailment of immigration. For them, immigrants are crucial to institution-building. "We're always looking for opportunities for people to join unions. That's our number-one reason for working with immigrants," noted AFL-CIO spokeswoman Kathy Roeder a few years ago. More recently, Jim Gleason, a Colorado-based United Brotherhood of Carpenters chieftain, defends his union's outreach program to illegal immigrants this way: "If you want to grow, you have to represent the people who are doing the work." In his state, the union's share of construction jobs has plunged from about 70 percent to 10 percent over the past three decades.

Union officials are looking out for themselves, but not their members or the American public. In a 2001 nationwide Zogby poll taken not long before the 9/11 terrorist attacks, 60 percent of union households thought amnesty was either a "bad" or "very bad" idea. And a recent *Time* magazine poll that showed 63 percent of respondents from all walks of life considered illegal immigration a "very serious" or "extremely serious" problem. Patriotism aside, there is a reason for most Americans' divergence from union leaders. Many better-paid union members sense, properly, that huge influxes of immigrants, even if successfully organized, will wind up undercutting union collective-bargaining ability.

Labor's strategy to ratchet up immigration indefinitely is self-defeating. Unions may acquire additional members and dues collections, but they will get a bumper crop of workers who are less skilled, educated and English-fluent than the overall labor force. These workers are replaceable. And replaceable workers, in whatever industry, are in no position to press demands. unless they engage in Justice for Janitors-style *sturm und drang* [turmoil]. The nation as a whole, moreover, will pay a heavy price in the form of more job displacement of the higher-priced native-born, further expansion of foreign-language enclaves, and more stage-managed political balkanization. That's not a legacy that anyone, least of all union officials, should covet.

"*U.S. employers . . . use the threat of plant closings, or actual plant closings, to keep unions out where they do not already exist and get rid of them where they do.*"

Corporate Off-Shoring Is Destroying U.S. Labor Unions

Kate Bronfenbrenner and Stephanie Luce

Labor researchers Kate Bronfenbrenner and Stephanie Luce have reported that the federal Bureau of Labor Statistics significantly underreports U.S. job loss caused by corporate relocation of production facilities overseas, the phenomenon known as offshoring. In this viewpoint, Bronfenbrenner and Luce present evidence that more than half of the jobs leaving the United States for Mexico, and 34 percent of the jobs leaving for China, are union jobs, striking figures in light of the fact that unionization in some U.S. industries is as low as 8 percent. The authors conclude that U.S. employers are systematically restructuring firms to eliminate union jobs and making it clear to nonunion employees that their jobs will be next if they attempt to unionize their

Kate Bronfenbrenner and Stephanie Luce, "Research on global production shifts, Research design and methodology, Union Status and US region of origin," *The Changing Nature of Corporate Global Restructuring: The Impact of Production Shifts on Jobs in the U.S., China, and Around the Globe.* Washington, DC: U.S.-China Economic and Security Review Commission, October 14, 2004, pp. 7–8, 36–41, http://digitalcommons. ilr.cornell.edu/cbpubs/15.

workplace. Kate Bronfenbrenner is director of labor education re-search at the School of Industrial and Labor Relations at Cornell University. Stephanie Luce is research director and assistant pro-fessor at the University of Massachusetts, Amherst.

As you read, consider the following questions:

1. What percent of firms that have moved jobs from the United States to Mexico, and from the United States to China, are closing union facilities, accord-ing to Bronfenbrenner and Luce?
2. According to the authors, how many union jobs were shifted out of the United States in the first three months of 2004?
3. In the authors' account, how did Continental Tire scare workers at its Mt. Vernon, Illinois, plant out of voting for a union?

There has been an explosion of interest among the general public in tracking the companies that are shifting jobs from one country to another. Examples range from CNN's "Exporting America" features on *Lou Dobbs Tonight* (2004), to the Washington Alliance of Technology Workers outsourcing website (Techs Unite 2004). While these organizations attempt to provide accurate listings of companies that have at some point shifted jobs and production out of the U.S., they do not tend to follow a rigorous research methodology to reliably capture when the shifts occurred, the actual numbers of jobs shifted to each country, and the characteristics of the compa-nies and jobs that are being shifted. Still, the groups highlight the increased public awareness of the practice of global out-sourcing of jobs and the policy implications of job disloca-tions for workers, unions, communities, business, and government. . . .

Union Status

In 2001 we found significant differences in the union status of companies shifting production from the U.S. to China, only 14 percent of which were unionized, and those shifting production to Mexico, 26 percent of which were unionized. In contrast, three years later, with private-sector union density now as low as 8 percent, we find that 29 percent of production shifts out of the U.S. are in unionized facilities, including 44 percent of firms moving jobs from the U.S. to Mexico and 29 percent of firms moving jobs to China.

Seventeen percent of production shifts to other Latin American countries and 15 percent of production shifts to other Asian countries were in unionized workplaces. It is only among the firms moving to India (7 percent) where we found unionization levels close to the national average.

[We also considered] the percentage of shifts by total jobs. These numbers provide an even stronger picture of the trends in global relocation. More than half of the jobs leaving the U.S. for Mexico and 34 percent of the jobs leaving the U.S. for China are union jobs, while, overall, 39 percent of all jobs leaving the U.S. are union. Even among the white-collar and high tech jobs moving to India and Latin American countries other than Mexico, the percent of union jobs is much higher than the unionization rate in those industries.

When we convert these percentages to numbers, we see that in January–March 2004, 12,511 union jobs left the U.S. for Mexico. In that same period, 2,833 union jobs left for China. Altogether, 19,086 union jobs were moved overseas in the first three months of 2004.

This change from 2001 to 2004 reflects the increase in production shifts among high-end manufacturing industries to China and other countries, but it also reflects the current labor relations environment. As documented in Bronfenbrenner's past research on employer use of plant closings and plant closing threats in the context of union organiz-

Outsourcing America

The labor movement has fought the flawed trade and tax policies of the 1970s, 1980s, and 1990s that rewarded companies for shipping American manufacturing jobs overseas. Today, we stand united in opposition to outsourcing away our best service-sector jobs as well. . . .

While off-shoring by companies wanting to exploit workers in other countries instead of hiring U.S. workers and graduates will be difficult to deter, public policies that aid and abet runaway corporations must change, and the U.S. must proactively develop a coherent and comprehensive employment policy. . .

Trade agreements must be fundamentally reformed to include enforceable protections for the rights of all workers—whether in manufacturing, agriculture, or services—to form independent unions, bargain with their employers, and reject child labor, forced labor, and discrimination. Trade agreements should also allow appropriate space for countries to implement legitimate tax and procurement policies that support job creation in domestically oriented production, and for countries to implement safeguards and other trade remedies in response to import surges and unfair trade practices in the services sector.

AFL-CIO, "Outsourcing America," March 11, 2004.

ing campaigns, U.S. employers are feeling increasingly emboldened to use the threat of plant closings, or actual plant closings, to keep unions out where they do not already exist and get rid of them where they do. In some cases, companies used the threat of an intended production shift to extract concessions from their unionized workers. For example, at the John Deere Des Moines Works in Ankeny, Iowa, in January 2004, the company announced plans to shift forty assembly parts jobs from Ankeny to Monterrey, Mexico. In the short term, no workers would lose their jobs. However, under the contract with UAW Local 450, the union had 120 days to prove that they could do the work more cheaply and more effectively than in Mexico. If they succeed the work will stay. If they fail, the forty jobs will be transferred to Mexico.

It is possible that our data overstates the proportion of unionized jobs leaving the U.S., given that our data on union jobs may be more reliable. However, it is clear that the absolute number of union jobs shifting out of the U.S. is quite high—almost 20,000 in three months. It seems difficult to deny a systematic pattern of firm restructuring that is moving jobs from union to non-union facilities within the country, as well as to non-union facilities in other countries. One example of this occurred at Continental Tire.

The Case of Continental Tire

Continental Tire North America is a subsidiary of Continental AG, a global auto parts and tire manufacturer based in Germany. As of mid-2004, Continental Tire North America had approximately 7,000 employees in six locations in North America: Charlotte, North Carolina (where its headquarters are located); Bryan, Ohio; Mayfield, Kentucky; Mt. Vernon, Illinois; Barnesville, Georgia; and San Luis Potosi, Mexico. Continental Tire went through some difficulty when it voluntarily recalled a half-million tires at the end of 2002 due to a mislabeling of tire pressure requirements. However, by May 2004, Continental AG CFO Alan Hippe announced "a positive dynamic in the U.S.," and strong sales growth including a 5 percent sales increase worldwide. Summarizing 2003, CEO Manfred Wennemer remarked, "Passenger Cars last year was the division with the highest growth rate, 8.4%."

Yet Continental Tire had already begun restructuring passenger tire production. In late 2002, the company notified the United Steelworkers of America (USWA) (which represents workers at most of the plants), that the Mayfield, Kentucky, plant was too costly and was no longer competitive. The company asked the union to come up with ways to reduce costs in the plant. The company then asserted that the union refused to work with them, and laid off two hundred workers in December 2003. The union claimed that it had in fact tried to negotiate with the company, but the company insisted the only way to save the plant was "to somehow cut $35 million from a $55 million payroll, and management had no proposals for how to do this."

In a March 30, 2004, conference call with investors, Wennemer stated that the company had reduced capacity at the Mayfield, Kentucky, plant, and that "a potential closure of the Mayfield plant is clearly in the cards." Wennemer went on to say that in addition to reductions at Mayfield, "we also reduced the headcount in the two headquarters and, more importantly we also . . . [began] the increase of production capacity in Malaysia and the start of building a new greenfield in Brazil. This is all in addition to the long continuing increase of production in our [San Luis Potosi] plant in Mexico." The next month, two hundred more workers were laid off in Mayfield. . . .

In late June, the company announced it would suspend production at Mayfield indefinitely and lay off more than eight hundred workers.

Meanwhile, the USWA had been engaged in an effort to organize 1,500 workers at the Mt. Vernon, Illinois, plant, the one U.S. plant that remained non-union. The union had held four unsuccessful elections at the plant since 1989, and another was scheduled for July 22–24, 2004. However, by mid-July the union began filing NLRB [National Labor Relations Board] charges, claiming that the company was intimidating workers, including announcing the potential plant closure in Mayfield as a way to scare workers into voting against the union. According to a *Business Wire* report, the company had already been charged by the NLRB with "massive labor law violations" against the USWA local in Charlotte, North Carolina, in 1999. The vote was held in July, and once again the union lost—though by only fifty-eight votes, its closest margin yet.

By the August 2 conference call, Continental managers were speaking about the Mayfield plant as essentially closed. CFO Alan Hippe noted, "You would surely have heard that we have an indefinite suspension of tire production in Mayfield in place. It will be done and finalized at the end of the year 2004."

On September 2, the company opened negotiations with the union. According to a *PR Newswire* release, the USWA presented their cost savings proposal to the company on September 17. They estimated that their plan could save the company $20 million a year. Continental Tire rejected the proposal. Nick Fletcher, vice president of human resources, remarked, "It is regrettable that these negotiations did not result in an agreement to preserve jobs at the Mayfield plant," but that the proposals "simply did not go far enough to address the cost disparity between Mayfield and our other tire plants." At the end of September, Continental Tire made the official announcement that they would permanently suspend tire production in Mayfield, Kentucky, and lay off more than eight hundred workers by the end of 2004. Meanwhile, the nonunion facility, Mt. Vernon, remains open, with the union organizing drive quashed, while Mayfield's closure serves as a stark reinforcement of Continental's threat to close Mt. Vernon if they ever were to choose a union.

| "Global companies require global orga-
nizing, global unions."

Corporate Off-Shoring
Spurs the Growth of Global
Labor Movements

David Moberg

The idea of global union movements has existed since the mid-nineteenth century. Twenty-first century dominance of manufacturing and trade by multinational corporations—the global economy—has revived that idea and mobilized global union federations (GUFs), David Moberg contends in this viewpoint. Moberg points to the International Trade Union Confederation (ITUC), an alliance of 168 million workers founded in 2006, as an example of unions' unprecedented solidarity and new focus on international organizing. Although international labor law and trade and economic agreements presently favor corporate interests, Moberg argues that unions do have some powerful tools to protect workers' rights—for example, the Alien Tort Claims Act permits workers victimized overseas by U.S. corporations to sue in U.S. federal court. David Moberg, a senior editor for the monthly news and opinion magazine In These Times, *researches the new global economy.*

David Moberg, "Solidarity Without Borders," *In These Times*, February 7, 2007. Reproduced by permission of the publisher, www.inthesetimes.com.

As you read, consider the following questions:

1. What two technological advances have made it much easier for workers around the world to work together, according to Moberg?

2. What cross-border differences does Moberg say divide rather than unify workers and stand in the way of global unionization?

3. How did unions cooperate in the 2001 cross-border campaign against the Canadian printing company Quebecor, according to the author?

With John Lennon's "Imagine" playing in the background, more than 1,000 leaders of service and technology unions from around the world gathered in Chicago in the fall of 2005. As delegates at the Union Network International (UNI) convention, they represented about 15 million workers in 140 countries. The challenge they faced was laid out in bold by the banner before them: "Global companies require global organizing, global unions."

It's an idea that's as old as it is new. Back in 1848, [Karl] Marx and [Friedrich] Engels exhorted the workers of the world to unite, and in the late 19th century, during an earlier wave of globalization, confederations of unions in similar industries—like metalworking—began to form across borders. But in the United States and elsewhere, the idea remains new and alien to many labor leaders, even as those same international union groupings—now called Global Union Federations (GUFs)—confront a seemingly borderless economy dominated by transnational corporations.

Despite the long history of global federations, no real global union exists. "For a union to exist at any place and any time, there are many preconditions," says Ron Oswald, general secretary of the International Union of Foodworkers (IUF), one of the most imaginative global union federations. "First workers [must] know there's a union, and employers [must] know there's a union. I'm not sure any worker or employer knows there's a global union. It's a brand, not a reality. International companies are clearly a reality. International unions have yet to become so.". . .

Unions Both Compete and Cooperate

The contemporary global economy presents labor with a double challenge in regards to global solidarity. On the one hand, corporations push workers into competition over who gets jobs and investment, especially in highly mobile manufacturing or digitized services. At the same time, unions, even in rich countries, realize that they can—and often must—work together to confront those corporations and to lift the standards of working conditions everywhere.

In November 2006, the 57-year old International Confederation of Free Trade Unions—the world's largest organization of national union federations—merged with a smaller world federation of unions aligned with Christian Democratic political parties, as well as several independent federations, such as the communist-oriented GGT of France. Stan Gacek, AFL-CIO assistant director of international affairs, calls it a "major quantum leap, in terms of organization of the labor movement on a global basis."

Guy Ryder, general secretary of the newly expanded federation, now called the International Trade Union Confederation (ITUC), says that the politics of the merger were as important as its size, roughly 168 million workers. "This would have been almost unimaginable even four years ago," Ryder says. "Unions saw the Cold War as an element of division in the labor movement, even 15 years after the end of the Cold War."

The merger also created a closer alliance between the ITUC and the GUFs. As a result, the GUFs will focus more on organizing and bargaining by industry and corporation, leaving broader political work to the ITUC.

"The key on global work is to figure out ways to do global grassroots action, not meetings," says Larry Cohen, president of the Communications Workers of America. "For a hundred years, too much has been about sending leaders to meet and dine together, which is great for building relationships, but we're looking for global events, ways for people to act together."

Global Unions' Most Important Tool: The Internet

The revolutions in communications and transportation that enabled corporate globalization—such as cheaper airfares and the Internet—make it easier for workers around the world to connect. Korean workers can send videos of their participation at a Haymarket rally in Chicago over their cell phones back to a rally of co-workers in Korea. "We couldn't even begin to think about doing the work we do without the Internet," says Christy Hoffman, an SEIU official who serves as the European-based organizing director for UNI's property services division.

Eric Lee, founder of the LabourStart Web site, which mobilizes labor supporters around global causes, says that the Internet greatly increases the speed and numbers of activists responding to a crisis—like a successful campaign to reverse the firing of an Irish union shop steward for wearing her union pin. It has also increased the involvement of grassroots activists. "International solidarity work has penetrated to the shop floor level," he says, "and hundreds of times as many people are involved in global solidarity work."

A Cold Splash of Reality

Unions are seeking other ways to meet global capital on a more level playing field. In January 2007, several unions—Amicus and the Transport and General Workers Union (T&G), two of Britain's largest unions; IG Metall (the giant German metalworkers union); and the Steelworker and Machinist unions in the United States—announced plans for a new "super union." The proposal is still just a "theoretical concept," says Steelworkers' International Affairs Director Gerald Fernandez, but other unions are also talking about forming joint cross-border unions. And the Farm Labor Organizing Committee already organizes in both Mexico and the United States to represent largely migrant workers in North Carolina and Ohio.

Yet a cold splash of reality is needed. Easier communication and the consolidating forces of global capital may help unite unions, but language, institutional structures, levels of economic development, national identity, strategic differences, and national labor laws and traditions all act as dividers. At a time when the former "international unions" covering neighboring countries like Canada and the United States continue to separate into national unions, creating global unions will not be easy. For the foreseeable future, the challenge will simply be to increase global cooperation and coordination.

Part of the problem is the weakness of what passes for global governance and labor law. Today, the most powerful global governance of the world economy comes from institutions like the World Trade Organization and the International Monetary Fund, which tilt against labor. Although it often appears that corporations write the rules of the new global economy, they still rely on governments to do their bidding. By using their economic and political power to change governments and laws, global unions can change those rules.

Labor unions around the world have agreed that international trade and economic agreements must include protection of labor rights. When no such protections exist, U.S. unions have increasingly used legal avenues to challenge corporations and both the U.S. and foreign governments. The AFL-CIO has taken cases to the ILO contesting the Bush administration's National Labor Relations Board decisions that restrict the right to organize. And Mexican and U.S. unions have filed NAFTA complaints about U.S. violations of the rights of Washington apple pickers and North Carolina state employees. The AFL-CIO also has used trade law to challenge labor rights violations in China and Jordan, but new free trade agreements have removed the threat of suspending trade preferences for violations of worker rights. And some unions have employed a powerful but controversial legal tool, the Alien Tort Claims Act. Used mainly by the International Labor Rights Fund—successfully against Chevron's slave labor practices in Burma—this law permits workers victimized overseas by U.S. corporations to sue in U.S. federal courts. . . .

Targeting Transnationals

The most important global work in recent years has been cross-border campaigning in support of strikes or organizing drives at particular transnational corporations. Most are so-called "comprehensive campaigns" that find chinks in the corporate armor where unions and their allies, usually non-governmental organizations like churches or worker rights advocates, can apply pressure. Such global support has been critical in high-profile U.S. labor victories, like the Steelworkers' battles with Ravenswood Aluminum and Bridgestone/Firestone, the 1997 Teamster strike against UPS, and UNITE HERE's campaign at the Brylane clothing warehouse (owned by a French multinational). Currently, the west coast longshoremen are working with Korean unions to help organize Blue Diamond almond workers in California, because Korea is a major market for the company, and the Mineworkers are jointly campaigning with Australian miners to organize Peabody Coal.

In most cases, U.S. unions ask their counterparts to pressure corporations with whom they have some clout. Western European union leaders, however, often do not understand how anti-union businesses are in the United States and are

Global Capital Demands
a Global Labor Response

The growth and concentration of transnational capital has fueled far-right political trends in many of the industrialized countries, including the U.S.

In the early years, the strongest trend in the U.S. labor movement was to channel anti-capitalist globalization sentiment into right-wing and jingoistic [nationalistic] directions. Some fell for arguments that pitted U.S. workers against workers in other countries and against immigrant workers. Japan bashing and "Buy American" campaigns mobilized xenophobic [fear of that which is foreign] attitudes. Global capitalist competitiveness was packaged as worker-against-worker competition requiring wage and benefit sacrifices to "beat the competition." . . .

Today there is growing recognition that global capital demands a labor response that is global. . . .

However, increasingly it is the specific global union federations, what used to be called trade secretariats, that are the center of building day-to-day working ties for global labor. These global union federations are built on specific industries such as garment and textile or metal working.

In the past, these forums were mostly for sharing information and national experiences in fighting and organizing workers in specific industries. Today, unions go beyond sharing information to coordinated action including [cross-border strikes]. And much of the new global solidarity takes place outside of the two world federations and their global union federations.

Scott Marshall, *"Labor in the Era of Globalization,"*
Political Affairs.net, *July 28, 2005.*

more accustomed to civil consultations with employers rather than confrontations. They have at times complained that the Americans wanted them to risk their close relationships with employers, without getting help in return from Americans.

"The criticism that Europeans and Brazilians have of Americans is, 'You're only into international solidarity when you're about to go on strike or negotiate or there's a plant closing. What about the rest of the time?'" says Ben Davis, Mexico representative of the AFL-CIO's Solidarity Center, which trains and supports unions in many countries.

But relationships are growing more balanced, and campaigns are becoming less reactions to crises and more a part of global strategies. "We've moved from global solidarity to global strategy," says Ginny Coughlin, UNITE HERE's global strategies director. "Instead of making lots of statements, we're making mistakes, running into obstacles, which means we're making progress. We've embarked for the first time in union history on a real cross-border organizing effort in hotels and hospitality."

Organizing on a Huge Scale

As UNITE HERE bargained in 2006 with U.S. hotel chains, it also supported a new community-religious-labor organization, London Citizens, which is working with the almost entirely non-union London hotel workforce. Besides helping British workers unionize, UNITE HERE wants to stop U.S. hotel chains from embracing this new London operating model—outsourcing room-cleaning to immigrants minimally paid by the room, rather than offering them fixed wage.

SEIU has recently ramped up its global organizing dramatically. It is working with two GUFs (UNI and IUF) on organizing the transnational corporate leaders in four industries—security guards, school bus drivers, janitors, and (with UNITE HERE) "multi-service companies" that provide food, laundry, and other services. Thanks to coordinated global union pressure, the three multiservice giants—Aramark, Compass, and Sodexho—have quietly agreed to terms that will make organizing their workers much easier.

"The huge consolidation [in global service corporations] has made it more possible to organize with fewer players," says Stephen Lerner, SEIU's property services director. If global labor can guarantee workers' rights to organize at each of these companies, there's an opportunity to organize quickly on a huge scale. Also, though the companies are global, the services they provide can't be shifted to low-wage countries, as with industrial or digital service work. "They can't move the buildings," Lerner says. "workers [can] support each other because they're not competing for the same jobs." Ultimately, he believes, there should be true global unions that match the scope of global companies. . . .

The development of these global campaigns creates complex webs. SEIU has at least 15 staff working overseas, mainly in Europe, training organizers and developing relationships with individual unions and the GUFs, which are all poorly financed and understaffed. SEIU also provided IUF with seed money for an organizing fund, which will be replenished by a share of dues from new organizing that the IUF assists.

The Steelworkers have begun developing "strategic alliances" with unions in Australia, Brazil, Germany, Mexico, and other countries. The Mexican union helped the Steelworkers in bargaining with companies like Alcoa and Asarco, which is owned by Grupo Mexico. And the Steelworkers have staunchly defended the union's leader, Napoleon Gomez, when the government removed him from his union office for leading a strike over mine safety.

"Mexico is one of our largest trading partners," says the Steelworkers' Fernandez. "If we can't take care of labor rights in our hemisphere, how can we do it in other hemispheres? We have a philosophical basis for assisting them. That's what unions are about. We also have self-interest. Strong unions in

Mexico, Canada, and the United States make it difficult for multinational corporations to exploit any of us."

Unpredictable Campaigns

Global campaigns can take on a life of their own. When the small Graphic Communications International Union (GCIU) asked the AFL-CIO in 2001 to help develop an organizing plan, they decided to target Quebecor, a Canadian-based transnational printing giant. With UNI's help, they formed a global conference of Quebecor unions and pursued an international framework agreement.

As the company resisted, unions around the world joined in shareholder actions, protests with religious leaders, in-plant petition drives, and global days of solidarity—even a sympathy strike. Governments and client corporations were pressured to threaten cutoffs of lucrative contracts. Organizers trained by Solidarity Center helped win victories in Peru, Chile, and Brazil, as well as two elections in the United States. The Teamsters, which incorporated the American part of GCIU, hopes talks will now revive the stalled campaign.

Simply campaigning more, however, won't be enough. Unions need to change both the global political climate and the rules of the global economy. In some parts of the world, particularly Latin America, unions recently have turned more to populist and socialist politics, says Cornell professor Kate Bronfenbrenner, who organized a landmark conference on global comprehensive campaigns.

The global labor movement needs agreement on its broad political agenda. As AFL-CIO Secretary-Treasurer Richard Trumka argues, workers everywhere are boxed in by policies that promote capital mobility, labor flexibility, price stability, and privatization of government. When taken together, those policies, at a global and national level, undermine workers' economic power and social welfare protections, make organizing more difficult and limit what unions can do even if they do organize or undertake global campaigns.

"Is the labor movement actually becoming more international, either with regard to employers in organizing and bargaining or in relation to governments in setting policy at both the national and international levels?" asks one high-level union official with extensive global experience. "That's a tough call to say there's been real progress." Yet today more labor leaders and workers around the world at least recognize the need for global unionism, and are looking for ways to give the old idea of worldwide worker solidarity a viable form for a new era.

Periodical Bibliography

The following articles have been selected to supplement the diverse views presented in this chapter.

David Bacon — "Iran's Fledgling Labor Movement," *Multinational Monitor*, vol. 26, nos. 9–10, September–October 2005.

Peter Bakvis — "Giving Workers the Business: World Bank Support for Labor Deregulation," *Multinational Monitor*, vol. 27, no. 4, July–August 2006.

David Brady — "Institutional, Economic, or Solidaristic? Assessing Explanations for Unionization Across Democracies," *Work and Occupations*, vol. 34, no. 1, February 2007.

Tim Costello — "Why Labor Can and Should Lead a Reassessment of Approaches to China," *Global Labor Strategies*, May 23, 2007. http://laborstrategies .blogs.com/global_labor_strategies/2007/05/ why_labor_can_a.html.

James Fallows — "Why China's Rise Is Good for Us," *Atlantic Monthly*, July–August 2007.

Steven Greenhouse — "Labor Coalitions Divided on Immigration Overhaul," *New York Times*, June 26, 2007.

Hugh McGoldrick — "Do Unions Have a Role in Global Social Justice?" *PSAC Social Justice Fund*, June 18, 2007. www.psac-sjf.org/en/news/article.cfm? articleid=10.

Harold Meyerson — "Unions Gone Global," *Z Magazine*, April 29, 2007. www.zmag.org/content/showarticle .cfm?ItemID=12699.

Renuka Rayasam — "Labor Unions Without Borders: Will Workers of the World (Finally) Unite? Leaders Say Yes, But Barriers Loom," *U.S. News & World Report*, July 8, 2007.

OPPOSING
VIEWPOINTS®
SERIES

CHAPTER 3

Should Wal-Mart Unionize?

Chapter Preface

In 1962, businessman Sam Walton opened a five-and-dime store, Wal-Mart Discount City, in Bentonville, Arkansas, and the rest is history. By 1970, Walton's company had 38 stores in three states and 1,500 employees. By 1987, there were 1,198 Wal-Marts employing 200,000 people. Today, Wal-Mart is the largest private employer and largest retailer in the world, with annual sales of $358 billion and 1.6 million employees. Its retail divisions include Wal-Mart supercenters ("hypermarkets" up to 260,000 square feet in size that sell grocery and nongrocery goods 24 hours a day), the Sam's Club warehouse chain, and 2,700 Wal-Mart International stores in 14 countries. By any measure, Wal-Mart dominates.

From the beginning, Wal-Mart's business model has been based on selling a wide variety of products at the lowest possible price. Its success has had profound economic impact; as journalist Bob Ortega observes, Wal-Mart's "way of thinking has become the norm, not just in retail, but in all businesses."

Wal-Mart's critics don't think this is a good thing. The retail giant has been scrutinized for business practices that, while enabling it to sell goods at consistently low prices, drive out competition, drive down its suppliers' prices, drive American jobs overseas, and drive its own employees into near-poverty by holding wages and benefits to a bare minimum. Its antiunion stance is among the most contentious issues. According to labor-issues journalist Liza Featherstone:

> Only countries with the lowest-cost labor can meet the low prices the company demands. . . . Wal-Mart sells 10 percent of all goods imported to the United States from China, where independent trade unions are illegal and it is notoriously difficult to monitor factory conditions. . . . But Wal-Mart makes the conditions so much worse than they need

to be, pressuring factory bosses to cut their prices, so those bosses have no choice but to make employees work longer hours for lower pay. . . .

The company has been equally successful in keeping unions out of its American stores, partly because it has the resources to fight organizers in the stores and in court. Featherstone gives this example:

> In February 2000, 10 meat cutters in a Jacksonville, Texas Wal-Mart voted 7 to 3 to unionize their tiny bargaining unit. Two weeks later, Wal-Mart abruptly eliminated the butchers' jobs by switching to prepackaged meat and assigning the butchers to other departments, effectively abolishing the only union shop on its North American premises. . . . In June 2003, a federal labor judge ruled this move illegal, and ordered Wal-Mart to restore the department and recognize the butchers' bargaining unit. Wal-Mart has appealed that decision, but of course, most of the original butchers have left the company, so whatever the outcome, Wal-Mart wins. . . . For Wal-Mart, going to court for violating labor laws is simply part of the cost of doing business.

Loyal customers and Wal-Mart employees object to this portrayal and argue that U.S. labor unions are the true bad guys in this issue, more concerned with increasing union revenues and political influence than wages, benefits, or workers' rights. Wal-Mart offers good value and good jobs, they say, both of which would be lost if the company is unionized. The viewpoints in chapter 3 debate the need for and resistance to labor unions in Wal-Mart, an issue with universally personal relevance when every week more than 138 million people shop at Wal-Mart.

> *"Wal-Mart has let America down by lowering wages, forcing good-paying American jobs overseas, and cutting costs with total disregard for the values that have made this nation great."*

Wal-Mart's Anti-Union Business Model Is Bad for Workers

Wake-Up Wal-Mart

Wake-Up Wal-Mart is a Washington, D.C.-based campaign sponsored by the United Food and Commercial Workers (UFCW) union that is highly critical of Wal-Mart's nonunion employment practices. In this viewpoint, Wake-Up Wal-Mart accuses Wal-Mart of hurting its workers in the United States and overseas by paying poverty-level wages, forcing workers to work without pay, offering little or no affordable health insurance benefits, and aggressively targeting employees who attempt to form unions, from illegally firing them to closing down stores entirely.

99

As you read, consider the following questions:

1. According to Wake-Up Wal-Mart, what was the average annual wage of a Wal-Mart sales associate in 2001, and what was the government's poverty line in 2001?

2. What percentage of Wal-Mart's 1.39 million U.S. employees were not covered by health insurance in 2006, according to the author? On average, what percentage of their employees do other large companies cover?

3. How did Wal-Mart respond to the unionization of its Jonquierre, Quebec, store in 2005?

Wal-Mart has become much more than just a small corner store in rural America. In the past 10 years, Wal-Mart has grown into the largest retailer in the world—number 1 among the Fortune 500—and is America's largest employer. With more than 1.4 million employees and over $10 billion in profits, Wal-Mart is a giant company with giant responsibilities. First and foremost, Wal-Mart has a responsibility to all Americans to set the standard for customers, workers and communities, and to help build a better America.

The truth is that Wal-Mart has let America down by lowering wages, forcing good paying American jobs overseas, and cutting costs with total disregard for the values that have made this nation great. Wal-Mart has needlessly exploited illegal immigrants, faces the largest gender discrimination lawsuit in history, forced workers to work in an unsafe environment, and—incredibly—broken child labor laws.

America's largest employer must reflect America's values. But, Wal-Mart will never change on its own. Lee Scott, Wal-Mart's CEO, mistakenly thinks he only answers to a few wealthy shareholders who own Wal-Mart stock. Lee Scott is wrong. Wal-Mart and Lee Scott must answer to the American people. . . .

Wal-Mart Wages and Worker Rights

A substantial number of Wal-Mart associates earn far below the poverty line:

- In 2001, sales associates, the most common job in Wal-Mart, earned on average $8.23 an hour for annual wages of $13,861. The 2001 poverty line for a family of three was $14,630.

- A 2003 wage analysis reported that cashiers, the second most common job, earn approximately $7.92 per hour and work 29 hours a week. This brings in annual wages of only $11,948.

Wal-Mart associates don't earn enough to support a family:

- The average two-person family (one parent and one child) needed $27,948 to meet basic needs in 2005, well above what Wal-Mart reports that its average full-time associate earns. Wal-Mart claimed that its average associate earned $9.68 an hour in 2005. That would make the average associate's annual wages $17,114.

Wage increases would cost Wal-Mart relatively little:

- Wal-Mart can cover the cost of a dollar an hour wage increase by raising prices a half penny per dollar. For instance, a $2.00 pair of socks would then cost $2.01. This minimal increase would annually add up to $1,800 for each employee.

Wal-Mart forces employees to work off-the-clock:

- Wal-Mart's 2006 Annual Report reported that the company faced 57 wage and hour lawsuits. Major lawsuits have either been won or are working their way through the legal process in states such as California, Indiana, Minnesota, Oregon, Pennsylvania, and Washington.

- In December 2005, a California court ordered Wal-Mart to pay $172 million in damages for failing to provide meal breaks to nearly 116,000 hourly workers as required under state law. Wal-Mart appealed the case.

- A Pennsylvania court, also in December 2005, approved a class-action lawsuit against Wal-Mart Stores Inc. by employees in Pennsylvania who say the company pressured them to work off the clock. The class could grow to include nearly 150,000 current or former employees.

- In Pennsylvania, the lead plaintiff alleges she worked through breaks and after quitting time—eight to 12 unpaid hours a month, on average—to meet Wal-Mart's work demands. "One of Wal-Mart's undisclosed secrets for its profitability is its creation and implementation of a system that encourages off-the-clock work for its hourly employees," Dolores Hummel, who worked at a Sam's Club in Reading from 1992–2002, charged in her suit.

Wal-Mart executives did not act on warnings they were violating the Fair Labor Standards Act (FLSA):

- Wal-Mart has known for years of a massive companywide problem of fair labor standards violations but did not take sufficient steps to address the problem. An internal Wal-Mart audit of one week of time records in 2000 from 25,000 employees had alerted Wal-Mart officials to potential violations. The audit found 60,767 missed breaks and 15,705 lost meal times. It also alerted Wal-Mart executives to 1,371 instances of minors working too late, during school hours, or for too many hours in a day.

- Despite this knowledge, Wal-Mart had to settle in January 2005 for violations that took place from 1998 to 2002. Wal-Mart agreed to pay $135,540 to settle U.S. Dept. of Labor charges that the company had violated provisions against minors operating hazardous machinery.

- In March 2005, Wal-Mart agreed to pay $11 million to settle allegations that it had failed to pay overtime to janitors, many of whom worked seven nights a week.

- The State of Connecticut, investigating Wal-Mart's child labor practices after the federal investigation ended, found 11 more violations. In June 2005, Connecticut fined Wal-Mart Stores Inc. $3,300 over child labor violations after a state investigation found that some minors lacked proper paperwork and were operating hazardous equipment at the stores.

Wal-Mart and Health Care

Wal-Mart's health care plan fails to cover over 775,000 employees:

- Wal-Mart reported in January 2006 that its health insurance only covers 43% of their employees. Wal-Mart has approximately 1.39 million U.S. employees.

Wal-Mart's health insurance falls far short of other large companies:

- On average for 2005, large companies (200 or more workers) cover approximately 66% of their employees. If Wal-Mart was to reach the average coverage rate, Wal-Mart should be covering an additional 318,000 employees.

Wal-Mart's health care eligibility is restrictive:

- Part-timers—anybody below 34 hours a week—
  must wait 1 year before they can enroll. Moreover,
  spouses of part-time employees [were] ineligible
  for family health care coverage for 2006.

- Full-time hourly employees must wait 180 days
  (approximately 6 months) before being able to
  enroll in Wal-Mart's health insurance plan. Managers have no waiting period.

- Nationally, the average wait time for new employees to become eligible is 1.7 months. For the retail
  industry it is 3.0 months.

**All of Wal-Mart's health plans are too costly for its work-
ers to use:**

- Since the average full-time Wal-Mart employee
  earned $17,114 in 2005, he or she would have to
  spend between 7 and 25 percent of his or her income just to cover the premiums and medical deductibles, if electing for single coverage.

- The average full-time employee electing for family
  coverage would have to spend between 22 and 40
  percent of his or her income just to cover the premiums and medical deductibles. These costs do
  not include other health-related expenses such as
  medical co-pays, prescription coverage, emergency
  room deductibles, and ambulance deductibles.

- Wal-Mart trumps the affordability of its new
  health care plan. According to Wal-Mart, "In January [2006], . . . Coverage will be available for as
  little as $22 per month for individuals."

- What Wal-Mart's website leaves out: Coverage is
  affordable, but using it will bankrupt many em-

Wal-Mart's Ruthless Anti-Union Stance

Thinking union? Get outta here! "Wal-Mart is opposed to unionization," reads a company guidebook for supervisors. "You, as a manager, are expected to support the company's position. . . . This may mean walking a tightrope between legitimate campaigning and improper conduct."

Wal-Mart is in fact rabidly anti-union, deploying teams of union-busters from Bentonville [Arkansas headquarters] to any spot where there's a whisper of organizing activity. "While unions might be appropriate for other companies, they have no place at Wal-Mart," a spokeswoman told a *Texas Observer* reporter who was covering an NLRB hearing on the company's manhandling of 11 meatcutters who worked at a Wal-Mart Supercenter in Jacksonville, Texas.

These derring-do employees were sick of working harder and longer for the same low pay. "We signed [union] cards, and all hell broke loose," says Sidney Smith, one of the Jacksonville meatcutters who established the first-ever Wal-Mart union in the U.S., voting in February 2000 to join the United Food and Commercial Workers. Eleven days later, Wal-Mart announced that it was closing the meatcutting departments in all of its stores and would henceforth buy prepackaged meat elsewhere.

But the repressive company didn't stop there. As the *Observer* reports: "Smith was fired for theft—after a manager agreed to let him buy a box of overripe bananas for 50 cents, Smith ate one banana before paying for the box, and was judged to have stolen that banana."

Transnationale Corporations Observatory,
"Comprehensive Anti Wal-Mart Info Digest,"
Beyond McDonald's, *April 2002.*

ployees. Wal-Mart's most affordable plan for 2006 includes a $1,000 deductible for single coverage and a $3,000 deductible for family coverage ($1,000 deductible per person covered up to $3,000). . . .

Wal-Mart's Foreign Manufacturers
Wal-Mart's Chinese factory workers are treated poorly:

- Workers making clothing for Wal-Mart in Shenzhen, China, filed a class action lawsuit against Wal-Mart in September 2005 claiming that they were not paid the legal minimum wage, not permitted to take holidays off and were forced to work overtime. They said their employer had withheld the first three months of all workers' pay, almost making them indentured servants, because the company refused to pay the money if they quit.

- Workers making toys for Wal-Mart in China's Guangdong Province reported that they would have to meet a quota of painting 8,900 toy pieces in an eight-hour shift in order to earn the stated wage of $3.45 a day. If they failed to meet that quota, the factory would only pay them $1.23 for a day's work.

Elsewhere workers producing goods for Wal-Mart also face appalling conditions, despite Wal-Mart's factory inspection program:

- Workers from Bangladesh, China, Indonesia, Nicaragua and Swaziland brought a class action lawsuit against Wal-Mart in September 2005 asserting that the company's codes of conduct were violated in dozens of ways. They said they were often paid less than the legal minimum wage and did not receive mandated time-and-a-half for overtime, and some said they were beaten by managers and were locked in their factories.

- A female apparel worker in Dhaka, Bangladesh, said she was locked into the factory and did not have a day off in her first six months. She said she was told if she refused to work the required overtime, she would be fired. Another worker said her supervisor attacked her "by slapping her face so hard that her nose began bleeding simply because she was unable to meet" her "high quota."

- In 2004, only 8 percent of Wal-Mart inspectors' visits to factories were unannounced, giving supervisors the chance to coach workers [on] what to say and hide violations. Wal-Mart claimed it planned to double unannounced visits by its inspectors but that would still leave 80 percent of inspections announced.

- A former Wal-Mart executive James Lynn has sued the company claiming he was fired because he warned the company that an inspection manager was intimidating underlings into passing Central American suppliers. Lynn documented forced pregnancy tests, 24-hour work shifts, extreme heat, pat-down searches, locked exits, and other violations of the labor laws of these Central American countries.

Wal-Mart and Worker Injuries
Wal-Mart cares little for the safety of its workers:

- In 2005, the United States Court of Appeals for the District of Columbia Circuit upheld a $5,000 fine against a Wal-Mart store in Hoover, Ala., for blocking emergency exits. The court upheld a decision by a judge who found that Wal-Mart was guilty of a serious and repeated offense.

• According to a *New York Times* report in 2004, Wal-Mart instituted a "lock-in" policy at some of its Wal-Mart and Sam's Club stores. The stores lock their doors at night so that no one can enter or leave the building, leaving workers inside trapped. Some workers reported that managers had threatened to fire them if they ever used the fire exit to leave the building. Instead, they were supposed to wait for a manager to unlock doors to allow employees to escape in an emergency.

• The West Virginia state workmen's comp agency placed Wal-Mart in an "adverse risk" pool because Wal-Mart had unusually high accident rates.

Wal-Mart takes a combative approach to workers compensation claims:

• Arkansas Business in 2001 described Wal-Mart as "the state's most aggressive" when it comes to challenging worker's compensation claims. The company "stands far above any other self-insurer in challenges to employee claims.". . .

Wal-Mart Anti-Union Policy

Wal-Mart closes down stores and departments that unionize:

• Wal-Mart closed its store in Jonquierre, Quebec, in April 2005 after its employees received union certification. The store became the first unionized Wal-Mart in North America when 51 percent of the employees at the store signed union cards.

• In December 2005, the Quebec Labour Board ordered Wal-Mart to compensate former employees of its store in Jonquiere, Quebec. The Board ruled that Wal-Mart had improperly closed the store in April 2005 in reprisal against unionized workers.

- In 2000, when a small meatcutting department successfully organized a union at a Wal-Mart store in Texas, Wal-Mart responded a week later by announcing the phase-out of its in-store meatcutting company-wide.

Wal-Mart has issued "A Manager's Toolbox to Remaining Union Free":

- This toolbox provides managers with lists of warning signs that workers might be organizing, including "frequent meetings at associates' homes" and "associates who are never seen together start talking or associating with each other." The "Toolbox" gives managers a hotline to call so that company specialists can respond rapidly and head off any attempt by employees to organize.

Wal-Mart is committed to an anti-union policy:

- In the last few years, well over 100 unfair labor practice charges have been filed against Wal-Mart throughout the country, with 43 charges filed in 2002 alone.

- Since 1995, the U.S. government has been forced to issue at least 60 complaints against Wal-Mart at the National Labor Relations Board.

- Wal-Mart's labor law violations range from illegally firing workers who attempt to organize a union to unlawful surveillance, threats, and intimidation of employees who dare to speak out.

> *"Just as Wal-Mart has been good for consumers and investors, it has been good for its employees and labor in general as well."*

Wal-Mart's Anti-Union Business Model Is Good for Workers

Richard Vedder and Wendell Cox

Richard Vedder and Wendell Cox dispute critics of Wal-Mart's business and employment practices, contending that Wal-Mart's entry into a community has several positive effects: Wal-Mart saves consumers money and expands their product choices (improving people's standard of living), pays competitive market wages, offers fringe benefits comparable to those of other retailers, and boosts employment. Vedder and Cox specifically argue that Wal-Mart stores are concentrated in small, semi-rural areas where wages are low, and that Wal-Mart workers are mostly unskilled: These two factors alone explain any differential between Wal-Mart average wages and average U.S. retail wages in general. Vedder is distinguished professor of economics at Ohio Uni-

Richard Vedder and Wendell Cox, *The Wal-Mart Revolution: How Big-Box Stores Benefit Consumers, Workers, and the Economy.* Washington, DC: AEI Press, 2006, pp. 91–99. Copyright © 2006 by the American Enterprise Institute for Public Policy Research, Washington, DC. All rights reserved. Reprinted with the permission of The American Enterprise Institute for Public Policy Research, Washington, DC.

versity and a visiting scholar at the American Enterprise Institute, a conservative think tank in Washington, DC. Cox is an international public policy consultant and principal of Wendell Cox Consultancy in St. Louis.

As you read, consider the following questions:

1. In addition to empirical evidence, what three logical objections do Vedder and Cox have to the "Wal-Mart employees are underpaid" argument?

2. According to Vedder and Cox, why is it irresponsible for Wal-Mart's competitor Costco to pay its employees higher wages?

3. What two significant fringe benefits does Wal-Mart offer employees that the company's critics fail to take into account when criticizing its compensation package, in the authors' analysis?

Labor unions and some others have long argued that Wal-Mart employees are exploited, receiving low wages for their labors. Compared with other businesses, Wal-Mart, or so it is argued, pays a smaller amount, leading in some cases to poverty for its workers.

Before turning to the empirical evidence, it should be pointed out that there are several logical problems with the "Wal-Mart employees are underpaid" argument. First, it is worth noting that no one is forced to work at Wal-Mart. The people holding jobs there do so voluntarily, and have the legal right simply to quit and go to work elsewhere. Situations today are not like a century or more ago, when workers of firms in small isolated towns could not easily travel to locations where other jobs were available, leading to what economists call "monopsonistic exploitation [exploitation of workers by companies that have a monopoly on available work]." Today, it is a rare situation where within thirty minutes of home there are not at least some alternative employers offering jobs with skill requirements similar to those at Wal-Mart.

Similarly, when asked if they want to have collective bargaining, Wal-Mart workers have consistently said "no." The employees themselves have shown little evidence of profound disenchantment or a sense of exploitation. While Wal-Mart management has clearly wanted to keep unions out, they have not actively coerced workers into staying out of them, or illegally tried to subvert the nation's laws with respect to collective bargaining.

Finally, retail trade has always been a relatively low-paying field. Jobs are, for the most part, unskilled in nature and do not require advanced educational training. Workers are paid according to their contributions to store revenues, which are typically relatively modest. Merely showing that Wal-Mart employees make less than, say, the average pay in all occupations says little about Wal-Mart's compensation relative to comparable firms in retail trade.

Wage Comparisons

With that by way of background, let us look at some evidence regarding Wal-Mart workers. The company asserts that, as of this writing in late 2005, "Wal-Mart's average full-time hourly wage nationally is $9.68 an hour." This compares with an average hourly wage reported by the Bureau of Labor Statistics (BLS) for those in the occupation group "service" in private industry in the United States of $9.14 an hour. The Wal-Mart figure exceeds the national average by about 6 percent. Yet the Wal-Mart figure is well below some other data showing an average wage in retail trade of slightly over $12 an hour. . . .

Wages are most relevantly compared to those of other workers in the labor market in which they are employed. Service industry employees in metropolitan areas typically make a dollar or so more hourly than the average for nonmetropolitan areas. Similarly, employees in low per-capita income areas typically have lower wages. Adjusting for these factors, it is probable that the Wal-Mart wage is noticeably higher relative to reported national averages.

Wal-Mart helpfully publishes average hourly wage data by state. As of this writing, average hourly wages vary from a low of $8.75 an hour in West Virginia to a high of $10.94 in New Hampshire. The New Hampshire average wage is fully 25 percent above that of West Virginia. To be sure, the geographic variation of Wal-Mart wages is less than for workers as a whole, reflecting perhaps in part the possibility that unskilled workers have less wage variation, and perhaps also some company policy implicitly setting a minimum wage that benefits workers in lower-paying states. Regression analysis shows a strong positive statistical relationship between Wal-Mart average wages by state and the state-average wages of workers in general—Wal-Mart is heavily influenced by local labor market conditions in determining its wage rates.

The point that Wal-Mart stores are concentrated in lower-wage areas, thereby driving down the reported average system-wide wage relative to national averages, can be demonstrated by a simple arithmetic exercise. . . . We compare the ten most "Wal-Mart-intensive" states in early 2005 (based on stores per one million persons, as listed in the 2005 *Annual Report*), with the ten least Wal-Mart-intensive states. We look at the average wage level prevailing in the state for all workers, according to Bureau of Labor Statistics data.

Wages are strikingly (26.4 percent) higher in states where Wal-Mart has a very limited presence than in states where it is relatively ubiquitous. An analysis that incorporates the nonmetropolitan-area orientation of Wal-Mart would no doubt further demonstrate that, even today, its stores are concentrated largely in rather small, semi-rural areas where wages tend to be low. Even if the average wage for retail workers were close to $12 hourly while Wal-Mart paid about $10 na-

Wal-Mart Fills 100,000 Jobs Per Year

Wal-Mart's wages and benefits are competitive in the retail industry. If they weren't, the company wouldn't be able to maintain a workforce of 1.2 million people, fill 100,000 new positions a year, or routinely attract thousands of applicants for hundreds of positions when new stores open.

In a recent survey, 52 percent of hourly Wal-Mart associates said company wages were better than those elsewhere. Just 23 percent said the wages were worse. In terms of overall job quality, 36.5 percent of hourly workers described their Wal-Mart position as "much better" than their previous job. By contrast, only 3.7 percent selected "much worse."

Americans for Wal-Mart,
"Issues," 2006.

tionally, most of that differential would probably be explained by the stores' uneven distribution across the nation's landscape. . . .

There are other issues involved in comparing the reported Wal-Mart average wage to national data. First, the Wal-Mart data are based on full-time workers. While the company asserts that, unlike most of the industry, a majority of its employees are full-time, there are still a substantial number of part-time employees, a majority of whom probably make less than the typical full-time employee. The Wal-Mart figure also excludes supervisory personnel working on a salary (not hourly) basis, who are generally paid more than the average of hourly workers. If both part-time and salaried workers were included in our calculations, it is our suspicion that the resulting average wage would likely still be at least in the $10 hourly range, and possibly higher—highly competitive with service industry employees generally.

Still other data leave us with the impression that Wal-Mart's pay for employees is not strongly out of line with the industry standards. To mention one source, data from the U.S. Bureau of Labor Statistics National Compensation Survey for some occupations common at Wal-Mart are compatible with the Wal-Mart average. For example, the national average pay in July 2003 for "cashiers" was $8.40 an hour. Even allowing for some increases since then, the current figure for cashiers is still no doubt below the Wal-Mart average wage. The average for "service occupations except private household" from the same survey was $10.40 hourly, slightly above the Wal-Mart norm, but probably not so after appropriate adjustments for local labor market conditions are made.

Criticism of Wal-Mart's Rivals

An ironic and even amusing recent incident helps make the case that Wal-Mart indeed pays its workers in line with labor market conditions. A nemesis of Wal-Mart, the United Food and Commercial Workers Union, went out to hire protesters at new Wal-Mart grocery stores (called Neighborhood Markets) in the Las Vegas area. One of the store managers noted that while the average rate of pay for Nevada Wal-Mart workers was $10.17 an hour, the paid picketers were only paid $6.00 an hour—with no benefits. Wal-Mart's fiercest union critic was hiring workers to protest Wal-Mart at compensation levels more than 40 percent lower than those earned by the allegedly oppressed Wal-Mart workers. And the UFCW workers did not receive 401K plans like the Wal-Mart workers, health insurance (like many of them), or the like. One of the walkers on the picket line revealed to a reporter that he once worked for Wal-Mart, noting, "I can't complain. It wasn't bad. They started paying me at $6.75, and after three months I was already getting $7, then I got Employee of the Month, and by the time I left (in less than one year), I was making $8.63 an hour." His comment illustrates another fact: the lifetime earnings of many Wal-Mart employees are enhanced through promotions, and many of the relatively highly paid management workers begin as rank and file employees earning hourly wages.

To be sure, while Wal-Mart appears to pay wages not greatly out of line with industry standards, the company does not claim to be the industry leader in providing high wages or benefits for its employees. Some unions have championed the role of Costco in that regard, as that company proclaims as one of its goals making its associates (employees) content and satisfied. Wages are said by some to be as high as $15 an hour on average. While we could not verify that claim, even if true it raises an interesting question. Is Costco paying more in wages and benefits than necessary to acquire reliable employees, and, if so, is it violating a fiduciary responsibility to its stockholders by, in effect, giving away some of the fruits of their investment? The return on stockholder equity at Costco is typically in the 10–12 percent range, well below the Wal-Mart norm and also below that of all American industry. If the reason for this is making payments to workers beyond those reasonable to maintain their loyalty, it is reducing the wealth of the owners of the company and the company's ability to expand its services to consumers (which provide them welfare in the form of consumer surplus) as rapidly as it otherwise would. Whatever gains are provided to workers are offset by losses in wealth and welfare to consumers and investors.

Fringe Benefits

A favorite line of criticism of Wal-Mart detractors is that the firm does not provide benefits for its employees. Especially egregious in their eyes is that Wal-Mart pushes health care costs onto the general taxpayer, which, aside from being callous and exploitive of its employees, burdens the taxpayer and gives the firm an unfair advantage over other firms that allegedly do not engage in this practice.

While complete data are not available to analyze these criticisms fully, limited information suggests that the charges are largely without merit. First of all, the notion that "Wal-Mart does not provide health care benefits" is simply fallacious. As of late 2005, the company was insuring nearly a million people, including 568,000 employees. While these plans require payments by individuals, they are heavily subsidized by the company.

One might note that Wal-Mart has a total of well over one million domestic employees, so it is true that less than one-half (slightly over 43 percent by our calculations) receive health benefits from the company. These statistics, however, are similar to those for American industry as a whole. While the proportion of all workers in private industry receiving health care benefits is slightly higher (53 percent), the proportion with wages of less than $15 an hour having such benefits is less (39 percent).

Not only is Wal-Mart not markedly different from typical employers of low-wage workers regarding health insurance, but it is extremely unlikely that a majority of its employees are, in fact, dependent on Medicaid, as some critics claim. Large numbers of employees are part-time workers who are seldom insured by employers, even in the public sector. Many, if not most, of these employees are secondary earners in households where a spouse or parent has family health insurance coverage. Some older Wal-Mart employees work at the company part-time to supplement pension income and are part of the Medicare program to which they contributed through their taxes before retirement (and also now while working at Wal-Mart). One study estimates that over 90 percent of Wal-Mart workers are insured in some manner.

Is it possible that some part-time Wal-Mart employees have such low incomes that they receive Medicaid? Of course it is, just as it is true for workers at Target, in hospitality businesses (where average wages are lower than at Wal-Mart), and for a host of other employments. But it seems unlikely that the proportion of Wal-Mart employees receiving Medicaid is as high as the proportion of Medicaid recipients in the total U.S. population (15–20 percent).

Critics of Wal-Mart's benefits program tend not to take into account a significant fringe benefit offered by the company that has greatly enriched some senior employees. Wal-Mart contributes to a profit-sharing plan that, with provisions for bonuses for good performance, can be a healthy addition to compensation, particularly if capital gain income is included. The company claims that a majority of its employees own stock in it, which no doubt contributes to an apparent lack of hard evidence that, as a group, Wal-Mart workers are generally unhappy with their employer. For more than three decades, Wal-Mart has been justifiably proud of this plan. As Sam Walton himself put it, "I guess it's the move we made that I'm proudest of . . . [and] without a doubt the single smartest move we ever made at Wal-Mart."

An additional benefit that is hard to quantify but nonetheless real is the 10 percent discount employees receive on merchandise purchased at Wal-Mart. For some, the discounted price of stock or merchandise could well be worth a dollar an hour or more.

All told, Wal-Mart currently claims it spends more than $4.2 billion annually on employee benefits. That is at least $3,200 per employee. If the average employee, including part-time workers, works thirty hours a week and earns $10 an hour, each earns about $16,000 in annual wages. Thus, benefits are equal to about 20 percent of wages, a figure that appears to be roughly in line with the average for American industry. Wal-Mart does not stand out as a company with unusual employee compensation and benefit practices.

Wal-Mart Treats Employees Fairly

Critics of big-box retail stores, most notably Wal-Mart, claim that these stores treat workers poorly. They cost jobs and offer substandard wages and benefits. A review of the evidence, however, provides very little support for that position. With respect to employment, the evidence suggests, if anything, that the expansion of the discount retail trade industry has been associated with a net creation of jobs in America. There is no reliable evidence that Wal-Mart, for example, has been a job-killer.

Wages and benefits have to be placed in the context of the labor market in which workers compete. As a general proposition, a majority of Wal-Mart employees are relatively unskilled and are working in an industry that historically has paid low wages relative to other sectors of the economy. The evidence suggests that Wal-Mart wage policies are not significantly out of line with industry averages. Moreover, the allegations that Wal-Mart dumps its health care costs onto the governmental welfare system appear to be egregious distortions of facts. Just as Wal-Mart has been good for consumers and investors, it has been good for its employees and labor in general as well.

> *"There's little secret to Wal-Mart's suc-*
> *cess. The company will simply do what-*
> *ever it takes to keep workers from or-*
> *ganizing."*

Wal-Mart Fights Dirty to Keep Out Labor Unions

Christopher Hayes

In this viewpoint, political journalist and social issues commen-
tator Christopher Hayes accuses Wal-Mart of using strong-arm
tactics that violate workers' rights and labor law to keep its
workers from unionizing. Hayes portrays Wal-Mart's practices as
ruthless intimidation, including spying on and illegally firing
employees for suspected union activity (which the company goes
so far as to define as "speaking in hushed tones to each other"),
closing departments and stores where organizing drives are
launched, and requiring employees to attend one-on-one pres-
sure sessions with bosses or corporate union-busting teams. Ac-
cording to Hayes, Wal-Mart conducts its antiunion campaign
with impunity and pays government penalties and legal fees
when transgressions are prosecuted because these costs are a pit-
tance compared to the costs of raising wages and benefits. Chris-

topher Hayes is a senior editor at the monthly news and opinion magazine In These Times *and a contributing writer at the Na-tion.*

As you read, consider the following questions:

1. How many formal charges does Hayes report have been filed against Wal-Mart for illegal antiunion practices since 1999?
2. How would the Employee Free Choice Act make it harder for employers to unfairly keep workers from unionizing, and why has such legislation failed to pass, according to the author?
3. How does Wal-Mart apply a double standard for its employees in Germany and its employees in the United States, according to Hayes?

There's a moment in Robert Greenwald's documentary, *Wal-Mart: The High Cost of Low Price*, that serves as a perfect metaphor for the entire battle between organized labor and the country's largest private employer.

Josh Noble, an employee of the Tire and Lube Express division of a Wal-Mart in Loveland, Colorado, is attempting to organize 17 of his fellow workers into a union. As the Na-tional Labor Relations Board (NLRB) election approaches, we see Noble with a United Food and Commercial Workers' (UFCW) advisor going through the list of employees, discuss-ing who's with them and who's not. Noble says it looks about 50/50. Later, the organizer cautions Noble that he may have lost the vote of his friend Alicia. "No," Noble says. "I've talked with her quite a bit. She's just kind of hard to read . . . I hang out with her on the weekends. But she's definitely into it. She's real strong." Cut to: Alicia Sylvia in her car. Management's putting the squeeze on and she's now equivocating. We know what will happen. It's like watching David sent out to battle Goliath, blindfolded. Without a sling.

Wal-Mart Strong-Arms Its Suppliers as Well As Its Employees

By now, it is accepted wisdom that Wal-Mart makes the companies it does business with more efficient and focused, leaner and faster. Wal-Mart itself is known for continuous improvement in its ability to handle, move, and track merchandise. It expects the same of its suppliers. But the ability to operate at peak efficiency only gets you in the door at Wal-Mart. Then the real demands start. The public image Wal-Mart projects may be as cheery as its yellow smiley-face mascot, but there is nothing genial about the process by which Wal-Mart gets its suppliers to provide tires and contact lenses, guns and underarm deodorant at every day low prices. Wal-Mart is legendary for forcing its suppliers to redesign everything from their packaging to their computer systems. It is also legendary for quite straightforwardly telling them what it will pay for their goods. . . .

It also is not unheard of for Wal-Mart to demand to examine the private financial records of a supplier, and to insist that its margins are too high and must be cut. And the smaller the supplier, one academic study shows, the greater the likelihood that it will be forced into damaging concessions.

Charles Fishman,
"The Wal-Mart You Don't Know,"
Fast Company, *December 2003.*

When election day finally rolls around Noble loses the election—17 to 1.

It's not just that Wal-Mart has been winning the ongoing fight with the UFCW, which has been trying to organize the bulk of the company's 1.2 million employees [since 1999.] It's that its dominance has been so absolute that even the small victories the union has scored have proved to be Pyrrhic [a victory that comes with a devastating cost to the victor]. In 2000, when seven of 10 butchers in a store in Jacksonville, Texas, voted to join the UFCW, Wal-Mart responded by announcing that henceforth it would sell only pre-cut meat in all of its supercenters, fired four of the union supporters and transferred the rest into other divisions. (Three years later, the NLRB ruled the decision illegal. Wal-Mart is now appealing [as of 2005].) And in May 2005, when workers at a store in Jonquiere, Quebec, voted to unionize, Wal-Mart simply shut the place down. "They wanted to send a message to every other store," says UFCW spokesperson Chris Kofinis, "'Don't you dare unionize.'"

By Any Means Necessary

There's little secret to Wal-Mart's success. The company will simply do whatever it takes to keep workers from organizing. "Staying union free is a full-time commitment," reads one of the company's training manuals. "[F]rom the Chairperson of the 'Board' down to the front-line manager . . . [t]he entire management staff should fully comprehend and appreciate exactly what is expected of their individual efforts to meet the union free objective."

Managers are trained to call a special hotline at the first sign of suspicious behavior, including "employees talking in hushed tones to each other." After the call, the company's notorious labor relations division headquartered in Bentonville, Arkansas, will swing into gear, often dispatching a company jet to the afflicted store, bearing members of its crack team of union busters. Management will convene mandatory meetings with each associate and screen anti-union videos.

Former managers, like Stan Fortune, who worked for Wal-Mart for 17 years and then went to work for UFCW, say the store also illegally follows union sympathizers and spies on its employees with cameras in break rooms. "One of their favorite tactics is to say, 'We need to freeze all raises in the store because it can't appear that we're bribing anybody,'" Fortune says in the film.

And then Wal-Mart will find a way to get rid of troublemakers. That's what spelled the end of Fortune's career as a manager at the company. In 2001 Fortune was managing a Wal-Mart in Weatherford, Texas, when his boss instructed him to fire an employee suspected of talking to the union. "I told him 'I'm not firing him,'" Fortune says. "'That's illegal' . . . He got in my face and said, 'You fire him or I'm going to fire you.'" A week later, Fortune was gone. "I filed for unemployment and the state found I was fired without cause. That's when I found out that means nothing in the real world."

Since 1999 the UFCW and others have filed more than 300 charges against Wal-Mart with the NLRB, accusing the company of, among other transgressions, firing employees for suspected union activity in violation of the Wagner Act. In a third of these cases, the local NLRB office has issued a formal complaint and attempted to prosecute the company, but it hardly matters to the behemoth because even if the full NLRB rules against Wal-Mart, the resulting penalties are a pittance. Wal-Mart didn't return calls for comment, but generally they deny ever breaking the law.

In April, the UFCW threw in the towel and decided to start from scratch. Instead of seeking to organize workers store by store, it launched WakeUpWalMart.com, a public awareness campaign designed to educate the public about Wal-Mart's business impact and negative community effects. A coalition led by SEIU, Democracy for America and the Sierra Club has launched a similar project called WalMart-Watch.com.

All Unions Are in Trouble

Wal-Mart deserves just about all the bad press it gets, and its recent commercials stressing what a gosh-darn great place it is to work would suggest that these efforts are having some effect. But because there's been so much focus on Wal-Mart's misdeeds, it's easy to surmise that the company is a kind of outlier, and that the rest of corporate America would never stoop to such techniques. This is simply not the case. "The right to organize in the United States is on the verge of extinction," says Andy Levin, director of the AFL-CIO's Voices@Work campaign. "Wal-Mart's not a bad apple—it's the very symbol of a rotten system."

A book-length report on U.S. labor practices released by Human Rights Watch in 2000 found that "workers' freedom of association is under sustained attack in the United States, and the government is often failing its responsibility under international human rights standards to deter such attacks and protect workers' rights." Certifying a new union local through an NLRB election, which requires emerging victorious from several months of active campaigning by employers, 75 percent of whom hire union-busting firms, has become so difficult that unions hardly even bother anymore.

"If you look at the historical trends, 50 years ago, an average of 500,000 workers formed unions through the NLRB process every year," says Levin. "And the number of workers whose rights were violated in that process, according to the NLRB, was generally in the high hundreds or low thousands. Fast forward to today. The private sector workforce is twice as large, but the number that organized through elections last year was 80,000. The number of workers whose rights were violated, according to the NLRB, is over 20,000. And that's literally the tip of the iceberg. Most people's rights are violated probably before there's a union on the scene to file a complaint."

Employers don't have to break the law to be effective. They can legally require supervisors to actively campaign against the union upon pain of termination and they can require employees to attend one-on-one pressure sessions with their bosses. "No other industrialized democracy allows this," says Levin. But even if they do break the law there are no punitive damages or large fines. In fact, employers simply have to give back pay minus what the fired employee was making at his or her subsequent job. "Many employers have come to view remedies like back pay for workers fired because of union activity as a routine cost of doing business," says the Human Rights Watch report. "As a result, a culture of near-impunity has taken shape in much of U.S. labor law and practice."

For several years, Levin and others at the AFL-CIO have been attempting to build support for legislation that would chip away at this "culture of near-impunity." The Employee Free Choice Act, which currently has 204 sponsors in the House and 40 in the Senate, would legally recognize a bargaining unit if a simple majority of workers signed a card endorsing unionization. It would also create binding arbitration for the first contract a newly certified union negotiates, and increase penalties for employer violations. Similar legislation has come close to passing in the past, but has often fallen victim to filibusters from corporate friendly senators.

Such legislation isn't necessary in countries where workers' rights are already protected. In Germany, Wal-Mart has bought out several stores that were already unionized, and they have stayed unionized. Since Wal-Mart isn't in the charity business, it's safe to assume those stores are quite profitable. In the film, Greenwald interviews workers there who proudly speak of health benefits and six weeks of paid vacation. One woman says she doesn't understand—why can't her American colleagues form a union?

It's a damn good question.

> "Millions of Americans have expressed disagreement with the smears against Wal-Mart by the UFCW and its accomplices by shopping there in record numbers."

Labor Unions Fight Dirty to Organize Wal-Mart

Thomas DiLorenzo

In this viewpoint, Thomas DiLorenzo portrays Wal-Mart as the victim in the fight between corporate and union interests. According to DiLorenzo, labor organizers know Wal-Mart employees don't support a union and know strikes would be unsuccessful because so many people would be happy to fill striking workers' jobs, so the United Food and Commercial Workers Union (UFCW) wages a "corporate campaign" of propaganda, slander, and anti-capitalist rhetoric designed to sway public opinion and legislatures and get the company to sign a union contract, involving as few employees as possible in the process. If successful, he concludes, this strategy would harm employees by making Wal-Mart less competitive, cost consumers much more money for products, and undermine free-market principles of

Thomas DiLorenzo, "The Union Conspiracy Against Wal-Mart Workers," *Ludwig von Mises Institute*, January 23, 2006. Reproduced by permission.

supply and demand. Thomas DiLorenzo is professor of economics at Loyola College in Maryland and the author of How Capitalism Saved America.

As you read, consider the following questions:

1. What are the two main tactics of a union "corporate campaign," according to DiLorenzo?
2. What does DiLorenzo call "the Big Lie" unions tell Wal-Mart employees?
3. Which groups does the author accuse of collaboration in unions' smear campaigns against Wal-Mart, either out of self-interest or as dupes of the unions?

Most of the commentary on the ongoing propaganda campaign against Wal-Mart ignores what is probably the most important aspect of it: It is primarily a labor union-inspired campaign against Wal-Mart *employees*, as well as the company in general. This is the essential truth of all union organizing campaigns. Historically, all of the violence, libel, and intimidation that goes along with "organizing campaigns" has been directed at competing, non-union labor, not management. The Wal-Mart campaign is no different.

Wal-Mart: A Victim of a "Corporate Campaign"

The propaganda campaign against Wal-Mart is what is known as a "corporate campaign" in the labor union literature. There are very few strikes these days in America; so-called "corporate campaigning" is the new form of organizing. Unions finally wised up to the fact that, while striking may be great fun, with all the name-calling antics, bashing in of car windows (of cars belonging to "scabs"), puncturing of tires, and destruction of company property, it rarely got them anywhere. In fact, if replacement workers are hired during a strike all union employees lose their jobs. Strikes increasingly became an all cost/no benefit proposition, which is why they are so rare these days.

There are several rationales for corporate campaigns. For one, they have been a way of unionizing a workplace without directly involving the employees in cases where unions know they do not have employee support. There have been many instances where unions have lost certification elections by very large margins, telling them that they have no hope of organizing a particular company's employees. Rather than giving up, however, they will frequently initiate a corporate campaign against the company. The idea is to use every means possible to impose costs on the company, forcing it to increase its prices; embarrass the company's management with a campaign of slander; and portray the company in the media as some kind of social outlaw. It is easy for unions to generate such publicity with the assistance of various economically ignorant, capitalist-hating "nonprofit" groups, from clergy to environmentalists. If the company gives up and signs a union contract, all the complaints disappear immediately.

One tactic is to issue thousands of complaints about the company to regulators, who must then investigate the complaints, forcing the company to spend huge sums on legal fees. In addition, the union will issue press releases about how many complaints there have been about the company, implying that all the complaints are somehow real and legitimate. This may cost the company some customers if the publicity is bad enough. In the 1990s the corporate campaign against the non-union grocery chain Food Lion caused the organization to shut down dozens of stores. (The company subsequently recovered as consumers discovered for themselves that the union's charges against Food Lion were bogus, but it still cost the company millions.)

In Maryland recently, the state legislature—which is totally in the pocket of the state's unions—passed a law forcing Wal-Mart to provide its workers with expensive, governmentally

Unions Want to Kill the Golden Goose

Attention Wal-Mart shoppers: If you are a union member, why should your dues be used to orchestrate a legislative campaign targeting the store at which you shop? Your dues money would be better spent on the discounted goods that you need. . . .

Recently the U.S. Department of Labor (DOL) set out rules requiring labor unions to disclose the amount of money they spend on politics, and this information is to be made available online. Anyone . . . can now go to the DOL website (www.union-reports.dol.gov) to find out what percentage of a union's member dues is spent on political activities . . .

A quick check of the 2005 LM-2 forms for the SEIU and UFCW reveals extensive spending on politics. . . .

It also reports that it put aside $500,000 to help organize Wal-Mart. . . .

The idea that private employers of a politically determined size have a social—and legal—obligation to provide health insurance coverage is at the heart of the "fair share" legislation that targets Wal-Mart. The political Left considers Wal-Mart an exploiter of workers in Red State America. But most Wal-Mart employees believe the alternative to working at Wal-Mart is a less-desirable job or unemployment. And most other Americans think Wal-Mart serves the American consumer by keeping its prices low. . . . To have state governments require the company to pay for health insurance beyond its current benefits would kill the goose that lays the golden eggs.

Ryan Ellis, "Behind the 'Wal-Mart Bill,'"
CRC Labor Watch, *June 2006.*

prescribed health insurance, something that will certainly drive up its costs and make it less competitive compared to unionized stores.

The ultimate goal is to get the company to sign a union contract without ever involving the employees, a process that labor scholars call "pushbutton unionism." So much for the fable of "union democracy."

The United Food and Commercial Workers Union (UFCW), the largest union in the grocery industry, has been at the forefront of many corporate campaigns and is the chief organizer of the campaign against Wal-Mart. It is no secret that Wal-Mart's grocery prices are very much lower than they are in your typical, unionized grocery store chain. The "problem" facing the UFCW is that unionized grocery store chains tend to be much more expensive than non-union grocery chains (and often much dirtier and less consumer-friendly in general). Thus, they have waged long campaigns against such companies as Food Lion in an attempt to drive up grocery prices—all in the "public interest," of course.

Hurting Consumers, Misunderstanding the Free Market, and Telling Employees the Big Lie

As long as there is competition by the superior, non-union grocery stores, the unionized stores cannot compete as well with their bloated costs and their low-quality goods and service. The unionized stores will lose business to their superior, non-union competitors and may even go bankrupt. The union will lose members and, more importantly, dues revenues. Thus, the role of the corporate campaign, if it is successful, is either to unionize the non-union stores so that they will become just as expensive and inefficient as the unionized ones, or at least impose costs on the non-union companies that will achieve essentially the same outcome.

In either case, it is a patently anti-consumer policy that can only harm the employees of the "targeted" company. Consequently, the whole idea of a corporate campaign is based on a Big Lie: that the union is somehow concerned about the well-being of non-union employees at places like Wal-Mart. In reality, the objective of the union is to force every one of those employees to either join its union (and pay its expensive dues) or become unemployed. This is true of all corporate campaigns, including the ones against Nike and other companies operating in Indonesia.

While the media may portray unions as collections of Mother Teresas, concerned only with the plight of poor Indonesians, the reality is that the real objectives of the unions is to throw every last Indonesian who is employed by Nike out of work, forcing many of them to resort to begging, stealing, prostitution, or worse. That way, competition for higher-priced/lower quality textile goods produced in unionized factories in America will be reduced or eliminated. And the unions pretend to take the moral high ground in this patently immoral crusade.

America's universities are filled with economically ignorant haters of the free market, so university campuses have become major forums for union denunciations of such companies as Nike, Wal-Mart, and others. Faculty and students claim to be concerned about "social justice," but they are simply being used as dupes by unions who are not at all concerned with justice of any sort. Rather, their main concern is increasing the coffers of union treasuries by driving non-union competitors from the market.

The great majority of today's college students may never learn the principles of supply and demand, or understand how many billions of dollars *annually* companies like Wal-Mart save American consumers (including their own families), but they are indoctrinated as freshmen that any "moral" person should hate Wal-Mart, Nike, and other "outlaw" corporations (as defined by the union movement).

Rallying to the Wrong Cause

Economically ignorant clergy often lend a hand in this union crusade to throw thousands of people out of work, lending an aura of "God's work" to this immoral and anti-social crusade. And of course there are all the other usual suspects—environmentalists, "consumer activists," trial lawyers, and Wal-Mart's higher-cost competitors—who are happy to be a part of such smear campaigns because it satisfies their own self interests (or fattens their wallets) as well.

So far, millions and millions of Americans have expressed disagreement with the smears against Wal-Mart by the UFCW and its accomplices by shopping there in record numbers. As always, the public has nothing at all to do with such anti-corporate campaigns, which are always the work of small groups of union rabble rousers, intellectuals, and pundits desperate to portray themselves as being "on the side of the people." The danger is if these opinion makers succeed in convincing enough politicians to follow the actions of the Maryland legislature, which is arguably the most economically ignorant group of legislators in America (I speak from experience, having testified several times before committees of these jokers). If this happens then the grocery industry will become less competitive, costing American consumers billions and destroying even more billions of dollars in shareholder wealth along with it.

Periodical Bibliography

The following articles have been selected to supplement the diverse views presented in this chapter.

Michael Barbaro and Robert Pear	"Wal-Mart and a Union Unite, at Least on Health Policy," *New York Times*, February 7, 2007.
Anita Chan	"Made in China: Wal-Mart Unions," *YaleGlobal*, October 12, 2006. http://yaleglobal.yale.edu/display.article?id=8283.
Anita French	"Wal-Mart Critics on Both Sides Blast Company," *Morning News (Arkansas)*, May 31, 2007.
Jeffrey Goldberg	"Selling Wal-Mart," *New Yorker*, April 2, 2007.
Parija B. Kavilanz	"Wal-Mart's Plan to Conquer the World," *CNNMoney.com*, March 29, 2007. http://money.cnn.com/2007/03/27/news/companies/walmart.
Kris Maher	"Wal-Mart Seeks New Flexibility in Worker Shifts," *Wall Street Journal*, January 3, 2007.
Stacy Mitchell	"Keep Your Eyes on the Size," *Grist*, March 28, 2007.
Carol Pier	*Discounting Rights: Wal-Mart's Violation of U.S. Workers' Right to Freedom of Association*, Human Rights Watch, May 1, 2007. http://hrw.org/reports/2007/us0507.
Robert E. Scott	"The Wal-Mart Effect," *EPI Issue Brief #235*, Economic Policy Institute, June 26, 2007.
Jeremy J. Siegel	"In Praise of Wal-Mart," *Kiplinger's Personal Finance*, January 2007.
Winston-Salem Journal	"Doing Well, Doing Good," editorial, July 24, 2007.

CHAPTER 4

What Is the Future of Organized Labor?

Chapter Preface

In 2006, a group of labor lawyers, historians, and activists formed a nonprofit resource center, Global Labor Strategies (GLS), to help labor and social movements connect to, cope with, and succeed in an increasingly global economy. The problem, as Global Labor Strategies sees it, is that the traditional model of a labor union is at a dead end:

> Unions are rooted in national laws, national institutional structures, national labor markets, and national customs. But the corporations they confront are global—roaming the world for cheap labor, market access, and fewer environmental and other regulations. And capital moves around the world with the speed of a computer key stroke.

> The result: Capital has outflanked labor. No matter how strong the national labor movement, no matter how high the union density, a union can be rendered powerless if a company moves abroad, or even threatens to.

Labor movements in every advanced industrial country face this problem, which GLS portrays as "a classic bad news/good news situation":

> The bad news is that corporate and capital mobility undermines unions around the world. The good news is that creates a common interest among workers and their organizations around the world facing similar problems.

GLS suggests three ways organized labor can reinforce cross-border worker solidarity and take advantage of what it calls "a popular backlash against globalization and the leaders of the world's largest companies." First, unions must stop trying so hard to protect workers at home by influencing international trade policy—regulating trade between nations is less relevant as corporations, supply chains, and finance go global.

Rather, labor should demonstrate the connections between globalization and its effects—job loss, environmental degradation, declining wages, and unsafe working conditions—and develop agendas for confronting corporations over these issues.

Second, unions must resolve the internal conflict that comes from trying to represent the interests of workers as a whole at the same time individual unions are trying to represent specific trades with specific (clashing) interests. Sometimes this tension pits unions against each other; sometimes it leads to paralysis on important issues. Either way, it reduces unions' effectiveness and fragments support.

Third, GLS argues, the new focus on organizing and recruiting millions of new union members will not save labor when employers can easily move operations and outsource work to avoid unionization or defeat a strike. The task is impractical in any case: Even if labor organized a million new members a year, it would take decades to increase private-sector union membership, now 7.4 percent, to levels approaching the 35 percent peaks of the 1950s, when unions last exercised significant power. Instead, labor organizers should develop broad-based campaigns that emphasize "extending basic worker rights to all workers whether or not they belong to unions . . . critical issues like global warming and real immigration reform . . . [and] new ways to forge solid links with labor movements around the world." The viewpoints in Chapter 4 further consider the prospects for labor unions in the twenty-first century and debate how best to safeguard and advance workers' rights.

> "The Old Unionism, organized labor in
> the private economy, is in irreversible
> decline."

The Decline of Organized Labor Is Irreversible

Leo Troy

In this viewpoint, economist Leo Troy argues private-sector trade unions cannot regain their power or membership strength. First, Troy maintains, industries and occupations have life cycles; once an industry matures or is replaced by new or different technology, it declines and dies out, and naturally the unions associated with it go extinct too. Troy argues that "the New Economy"— mostly high-tech and service industries whose employees either have little history of organizing or see little need for unions—is replacing "the Old Economy"—manufacturing and heavy industries whose blue-collar workforce was the backbone of the union movement. The New Economy, Troy argues, is global, and simply too competitive for unions to survive except in the public sector, because only governments are immune to market competition. Second, he makes a key distinction between employees wish for union representation and their willingness to pay for that service: Today, he concludes, the Western postindustrial workforce

Leo Troy, "Twilight for Organized Labor," *Journal of Labor Research*, vol. 22, Spring 2001, p. 245. Copyright © 2001 George Mason University. Reproduced by permission.

doesn't want unions enough to pay for them. Leo Troy is profes-
sor of economics at Rutgers University in Newark, New Jersey,
and the author of Twilight of the Old Unionism.

As you read, consider the following questions:

1. What extinct unions does the author associate with "ancient" industries that naturally died out, and which three modern unions does he argue will share the same fate?

2. According to Troy, why would new pro-union labor laws be unable to reverse private-sector union decline?

3. How does Troy define "the New Unionism," and what does he predict its primary role will be?

The "twilight of organized labor" means that I expect unionism in the private sector, hereinafter the "Old Unionism," will not recover either the membership or the market share it had in the recent or historical past. The term "twilight" does not mean the extinction of private-sector unionism; to the contrary, it assumes that private unions will remain a key factor in determining working conditions in several important industrial sectors, notably auto and steel manufacturing, and transportation.

At the beginning of the new century, the membership of the Old Unionism is 9.4 million, almost 50 percent below its record high of 17 million in 1970. Its market share, or density, shrank from a record high of 36 percent in 1953 to 9.4 percent in 1999. These staggering losses extend across all private industries and, in fact, industrial densities now range below those of the depression years of the 1930s. State data portray the same picture without exception. Individual unions, once giants with hundreds of thousands of members and hundreds, even thousands of locals and district organizations, have shed huge numbers of members and subsidiary organizations. As a defensive measure, union mergers have increased rapidly. On the horizon is the largest ever, that of the Auto Workers, the Steelworkers, and the Machinists.

Meanwhile, there is no evidence of a turnaround either in membership or density. Since peaking in 1970, membership increased year to year only twice, in 1993–1994 and 1998–1999, and both gains were inconsequential. The density of the private sector has declined without interruption since peaking in 1953, and can be expected to continue to decline in the next decade.

Unions' Changing Function

The Old Unionism's slide into the twilight zone has altered what unions do and why. Foremost is the union movement's redirection from emphasizing its trade union function—organizing the unorganized—to political action. Although unions have always engaged in political activity, the current effort marks a new high. It began with the AFL-CIO's success in securing the nomination of Walter Mondale as the Democratic Party candidate in 1984, escalated with the nomination Bill Clinton in 1992 and 1996, and has been extended by the endorsement of Al Gore in the presidential election of 2000.

Unions' current accentuation of political activity has also translated into large financial and in-kind contributions to Democratic presidential and congressional candidates. Its preeminence over organizing is reflected in the still tepid outlays and unimpressive results in organizing. On the other hand, during the 1995–1996 presidential cycle period, the Federal Election Commission reported that unions' PAC disbursements totaled virtually $100 million. Most expenditures are funded from members' dues, most of which are compelled under union and agency shop agreements. When union members, who number more than 16 million, were asked to contribute voluntarily, they donated a total of $243 thousand in that election cycle—an average of $.02 per member. The minuscule voluntary cash political contribution clashes with the claim of the unions' leadership that it has the members' support for its political endorsements. It also implies justification for legislation which would require unions to obtain the authorization of members in order to spend union dues for political purposes. I have argued before the Senate Committee on Rules and Administration and the Subcommittee on Oversight of the House Ways and Means Committee that the unions' in-kind contributions far outweigh their cash outlays. On the basis of what I call a political multiplier (paralleling the Keynesian investment multiplier), I estimated that in the presidential cycle period [of] 1995–1996, unions' in-kind contributions could have been worth $300 million.

While the market is driving the Old Unionism into the twilight zone, its descent has generated other economic consequences—increased competition in labor and product markets. In the labor market, it has reversed the compression of skilled/non-skilled wage differentials which collective bargaining had narrowed: "By equating pay across workers within a market, [unions'] standard rate policies raise the pay of otherwise lower-paid workers more than otherwise higher-paid workers." Hence, instead of increasing wage inequality, as some academics have argued, markets have reversed union-imposed wage inequality. The weakening of collective bargaining also has shifted pattern settlements toward terms based on local market conditions. Far more important, individual representation, now governing more than 90 percent of the labor market, determines the conditions of employment.

Because of the weakening of the Old Unionism, product markets have also become more competitive, and the unions' opposition to free trade has mounted commensurately, as exemplified by the extension of Permanent Normal Trade Relationship (PNTR) to China and their previous opposition to NAFTA. The weakening of the Old Unionism has also contributed to the price and wage stability of the last decade and to increased consumer choice.

Another consequence of the twilight zone has been the sharp reduction in the number of strikes, time lost, and an increase in the number of strikes which unions either lost or gained little. The BLS [Bureau of Labor Statistics] reported that all measures of major work stoppages in 1999 were at or below the lowest levels recorded in the 53-year-old series. Industrial peace has doubtless contributed to the increased productivity which characterized the 1990s.

The twilight of the Old Unionism is also transforming the character of the union movement. Historically, organized labor has been dominated by the Old Unionism in the number of members and in philosophy. Its decline coupled with the rise of public sector unionism, hereinafter the "New Unionism," will transform the character and philosophical perspective of organized labor. The most important realignment will be the enhanced power of the teachers' unions, the National Education Association and the American Federation of Teachers, within the union movement. It is likely that these two organizations will merge in the near future to become the world's largest union, with a membership exceeding 3.5 million. The new union will affiliate with the AFL-CIO (the AFT is an affiliate; the NEA is currently independent) and, I predict, will supply the leadership of the Federation in the early years of the new century. The new labor organization will also alter the philosophy and policies of the union movement by moving it further to the political left.

Union Decline Is International

The U.S. is not unique in the decline of the Old Unionism; it has waned in all G-7 nations [Canada, France, Germany, Great Britain, Italy, Japan, and the U.S. G-8 nations include Russia]. Recently, the International Labour Office reported that "[i]n a large number of countries around the globe, trade unions have experienced a considerable drop in membership over the past decade ... [and that] the proportion of union members in the labour force has [also] declined, sometimes sharply, almost everywhere over the past ten years."

The U.S. led the way and its descent has been deeper than in other countries.

In Great Britain, the ancestral home of trade unionism, total membership at the end of 1997 was the lowest since 1945. In much of the period, if not most, the Labour Party, the unions' close political alter ego, held power including the years since Blair became Prime Minister in 1997. Over the decade. 1989–1999, total membership (private and public combined) in Britain shrunk nearly 1.9 million members, a decrease of 20.7 percent. In the U.S., total membership fell by just under 800 thousand, coincidentally, also by 20.7 percent.

Density among all employees in Britain declined from 34 percent in 1989 to 27 percent in 1998. Separate public and private data, for which there are figures only from 1993 to 1998, show that the decline in density affected not just the private sector, as might be expected, but the public sector as well. Public density fell from 63 to 61 percent in 1998, while private density decreased from 24 to 19 percent.

Japan, home to the world's second largest economy, has seen its unionization rate for wage and salaried workers decline from 29 percent in 1985 to 19 percent in 1995. But the Japanese plunge is larger when compared to 1950 when it stood at 46 percent. Strikes have virtually disappeared since peaking in 1970 paralleling experience in the U.S.

In Europe, (the united) Germany's density among wage and salaried workers fell from 35 to 29 percent over the four years 1991 to 1995. In France, the density declined from 14.5 to 9.1 percent among wage and salaried workers, 1985–1995. Italy's rates also declined. 47.6 to 44.1 percent, 1985–1994. Even the Scandinavian countries reported declines, although their densities remain high. However, analysts reporting on the Scandinavian unionism typically neglect to inform readers that the unions administer government social insurance programs, thereby virtually guaranteeing high membership and high density rates. In a real sense, the unions there are instruments of the state, because access to the state social programs is through the unions. The high correlation between these programs and unionism is visible from Israel's recent experience. Once stripped of the administration of health care, either completely or in part, union membership in Israel dropped sharply. The statistics are startling. Because the Israeli statistics for 1985 included pensioners together with active union membership, density plummeted from 126 [!] percent of wage and salaried workers in that year to 23 percent in 1995.

Of all the G-7 countries, Canada is probably the most interesting in tracking the international decline of the Old Unionism because its system of industrial relations and trade union experience have frequently been invidiously compared to the American. Contrary to the conventional wisdom, Canada has not escaped the "American disease"—decline in private unionism, membership, and density. I have shown that in Canada the market share of private unionism peaked as early as 1956, at 34 percent, three years after the American (1953), and that membership peaked about 1979–1980, nearly a decade after the peak in the U.S. Other analysts contrasting the U.S. and Canada were essentially comparing two dissimilar union movements, the American being predominantly private and the Canadian overwhelmingly public.

Over the last three years, Statistics Canada began to correct its classification of private and public employment and unionism, approaching the classification used by the author. Thus, its data for 1997, 1998, and the first six months of 1999 show private membership and market share at levels far below what the conventional wisdom had believed. Moreover, if Quebec were deducted from the total (because its unique la-

Fewer Unions? No Problem

Maybe unions aren't so crucial to worker well-being. When more than 90% of the private-sector labor force isn't unionized, why do 97% of us earn above the minimum wage? If our bargaining power is so pitiful, why don't greedy employers exploit us and drive wages down to the legal minimum?

The simple answer is that bargaining power comes from having alternatives. Even in the absence of unions, employers have to treat workers well to attract and keep them. In a workplace as dynamic as that of the United States, where millions of jobs are destroyed and created every quarter, a company's ability to exploit workers is greatly limited by how easy it is to find another job.

Russell Roberts, "Workers Are Fine with Fewer Unions,"
LA Times.com, *February 17, 2007.*

bor laws and practices make it distinct from the rest of Canada), Canadian unionism would parallel the American more closely.

In an earlier study, I reported that Canadian private-sector density had skidded from 25.7 percent to 20.7 percent, a decline of nearly one-fifth, over the decade 1975–1985. For 1990, I estimated Canadian private density at 18 percent. . . .

Even Canadian data of total union membership indicate that private unionism has been declining. The series which reports total membership and density historically (since 1911), shows that density in 1999 (25.7 percent) is well below that of two decades ago, 1980 (29.2 percent). The figures also indicate that public-sector organization has also probably peaked; peak membership of all unions was tallied in 1992.

Unions in the other G-6 countries reacted to decline in the same way as in the U.S.—to consolidate: ". . . many European unions have lost members for years and hope to pool resources to cope with financial difficulties." But will these amalgamations be able to address the different and often conflicting interests of a diverse membership?

Why the Old Unionism
Is in the Twilight Zone

Structural changes in the markets, increased competition, global and domestic, in other words, the New Age of Adam Smith, and employee opposition to unionism are the principal ingredients involved in the decline of unionism across G-7 countries. Not all factors are of equal weight in each nation. In the U.S. and Canada, employees' opposition to collective bargaining probably ranks higher than in European countries and Japan. . . .

Structural changes in manufacturing also made the U.S. labor market different from Canadian and European countries. In the U.S. they were more comprehensive than those in the other G-6 countries. The principal changes within manufacturing over the last three decades have been the increasing substitution of high tech for traditional manufacturing output and employment. These were accompanied by an enormous growth in professional and technical occupations which, in turn, reduced the relative importance, and in some instances, the absolute number of blue-collar jobs, the bedrock of unionism in manufacturing.

These industrial and occupational exchanges are a continuation of long-run developments initiated by the industrial revolution and are inimical [hostile] to the Old Unionism. Long-run changes in manufacturing, as in other industries, are the product of the economic life-cycles: [According to W.C. Mitchell in 1934] "once an industry has ceased to advance it soon begins to decline" and over time the life histories of industries tend to become shorter: "[A]n increase in the birth-rate of new products means an increase in the death-rate among old products and a decline in the average life-span of individual industries." In his study of manufacturing, Fabricant called attention to "young industries, whose output shoots up quickly . . . [whose] employment [also] expands, most often rather rapidly," while, "[d]uring the mature phase of an industry's development output expands slowly, if at all, . . . [and] jobs decrease unless the length of the working week is reduced sufficiently to offset the decline." As the exchange of high tech for older manufacturing industries unfolded, it was misrepresented as the deindustrialization of America when, in fact, it epitomized the secular industrial changes detailed by the studies of Arthur F. Burns and Solomon Fabricant.

Naturally, unions associated with mature and declining industries share their fate. Unable to cope with the changes in the composition of what is produced and how, membership in the Old Unionism has sagged across all G-7 countries. The most dramatic example of what long-run structural change has meant to unionism is a brief roll call of unions, now extinct, once associated with the rise and fall of industries and occupations: Elastic Goring Workers, Carriage Workers, Chandelier Workers, Stogie Makers, Sheep Shearers, Mule Spinners, Broom and Whisk Makers, Tack Makers, Sawsmiths, and Gold Beaters, to name a few from the "ancient" past. In this century, consider what has befallen the United Mine Workers of America, railway unionism, and most recently the auto and steel unions. At the end of World War II, the UMW numbered about 600 thousand members; current union membership in coal mining is 26 thousand. Total railway union membership is 198 thousand at this time with a market share of 66 percent. Unpublished figures on railway unionism which the author prepared many years ago at the NBER put membership at just under 1.1 million members, with employment on Class I Railways at 1,418,000, and density at 76 percent in 1947.

For the labor market as a whole, Freeman and Medoff calculated that structural change could account for "72 percent of the observed decline" in the U.S. density over the quarter century 1954 to 1979. But then they rejected their own findings, because, they claimed, the same structural shift had occurred "in virtually all major western economies" and without similar declines in density. Therefore, they concluded that a factor other than structural change was responsible for the decline in the U.S., namely, employers' opposition. Like the pied piper of Hamelin, the employers' opposition explanation soon attracted and has retained a legion of followers.

However, contrary to Freeman and Medoff's assessment, neither Canada, which they had singled out as especially meaningful, nor any of the other G-6 countries underwent the same structural change as the U.S. Furthermore, when they did experience structural changes in the labor market, the changes [came] well after those in the U.S. Even more important, in the U.S. the switch was dominated by private services and was accompanied by a huge growth in associated professional, technical, and managerial occupations. Freeman and Medoff and the conventional wisdom in general, ignored leads and lags in structural changes, even though leads and lags in labor markets translate into leads and lags in union trends.

Foreign exchange rates also contributed to the structural changes in the American labor market, especially in the 1980s [as Little writes]: "From 1979 to 1985, as the [U.S.] dollar appreciated and structural change accelerated, U.S. labor resources shifted out of mature industries and production jobs most susceptible to import competition and toward the service-oriented manufacturing jobs in which the United States had a comparative advantage." Exchange rates have played a similar role during the 1990s.

The scope of the market is yet another structural factor separating the U.S. from the other G-7 countries. The U.S. is the largest free market in the world as well as the world's largest trading nation. As such it exemplifies Adam Smith's tenet that the division and specialization of labor and product markets depend on market size. (This was one of the reasons which led him to recommend a policy of free trade.) Consequently, to compare structural change in Canada to the U.S. is misleading, since California alone matches the entire Canadian labor market.

Structural change also reflects the differential growth rate between union and nonunion industries. Unorganized industries are typically high-tech manufacturing and in the service sector, although there are a number in the older industrial sector which are innovators, as for example, the Nucor Steel Company. These industries and companies are characterized by employment growth, while unionized industries and companies are characterized by slow growth or loss of employment. Thus, in contrast to the conventional assessment of the effect of structural change on Canadian unionism—that there was little or none—Long reported that "about two-thirds of the loss in union density during 1980–85 resulted from poor employment performance of established union firms relative to nonunion firms, with the remainder due to factors such as a higher rate of closures among union plants combined with a failure to organized a commensurate number of new firms."

Comparing union to nonunion Canadian firms in manufacturing, Long found that between 1980 and 1985, total employment in nonunion manufacturing firms grew 23.3 percent, while unionized firms lost 12.9 percent. These results were paralleled in nonmanufacturing firms: "unionized firms managed to eke out an increase in their total employment of less than 1 percent over the five years [1980–1985] . . . [while] nonunion firms enjoyed a 15.4 percent increase in total employment." Similar findings for the U.S. over the past quarter century were recently reported by Farber and Western: "most of the decline in union membership rate is due to differential employment growth rates . . . between the union and nonunion sectors."

In the clash over the role of structural change and its consequences for unionism, Freeman and Medoff, and those who adopted their analysis of union decline, mishandled the statistics of unionism and employment of Canada and the other G-6 countries. When they (and others) asserted that Canada and other major industrial nations had experienced the same structural change from goods to services, but had not suffered the American disease of union decline, they relied on official data which combined public with private employment and union membership, concealing the decline of private unionism, the nature of structural change, the importance of government services in their labor markets, and the connection of structural change to the decline of the Old Unionism

The New Age of Adam Smith and Public Policy

Paralleling the conventional view that structural change had little impact on the decline of private unionism, the conventional wisdom recommended new pro-union labor laws to reverse the decline of the Old Unionism. Paul Weiler, a pioneer in that recommendation, adhered to it until he accepted the futility of such a policy being adopted. He then switched to urging the adoption of compulsory works councils: "it is necessary to take away from the employees (and also the employer) the choice about whether such a participatory mechanism [works councils] will be present . . ." with the right "of internal participation in a specified range of decisions in all enterprises" (Weiler, 1990, p. 282). However, this proposal has no more chance of success in Congress than his previous recommendation: adoption by the U.S. of Canadian style labor law. That recommendation was flawed because he believed that Canadian labor law had enabled private-sector unionism in Canada to escape the American disease of decline. However, as I demonstrated here and elsewhere, labor law did not prevent the Old Unionism from sliding in Canada.

Nevertheless, persuaded by academics and unions, the Clinton-Gore Administration, acting on the view that an amended NLRA would help unions, appointed the Commission on the Future of Labor-Management Relations (the Dunlop Commission) in 1994 to make recommendations to amend the NLRA. However, that expectation was aborted by the election of a Republican majority in the House of Representatives and the reelection of a Republican majority in the Senate in 1994. Even had such legislation been enacted, the data on Canada demonstrate that the tide of competitive forces and structural change in labor markets have pared the Old Unionism there as elsewhere despite very pro-union labor policies. In fact, Canadians referred to their labor policies as "super Wagnerism" to demonstrate how much their policies went beyond the original American law to promote unionism. Just as markets undermined the monopoly power of labor organizations, they have also "repealed" the National Labor Relations Act and "super Wagnerism" in Canada.

Only in the public labor markets which are virtually immune to competitive forces have unions been able to organize and to maintain a stable membership. Public employers' role in labor relations is virtually a mirror image of employers in the private economy, but the impact of each is not symmetrical. Private employers oppose the unionization of their employees for competitive reasons, while most public employers often promote unionism for political reasons. However, it is questionable whether private employers' opposition to unionism is as effective in stymying organization as is public employers' encouragement of unionization.

A preeminent example of a public employer's interference to promote the organization of the public's employees was the unionization of Los Angeles County's 70 to 80 thousand home care workers in February 1999. Because of the County's actions, the Service Employees International Union was able to enroll the County's home care workers after more than a decade of failure. If a private employer engaged in the same practices as Los Angeles County, it would [be] declared guilty of an unfair labor practice, and the Service Employees' subordinate union would have been declared a company-dominated labor organization and disestablished under the National Labor Relations Act.

In the private labor market employers' opposition became the hallmark of many analysts' explanation of the decline of the Old Unionism (following the lead of Weiler), even though its impact quantitatively has never been demonstrated. Moreover, its advocates seldom explain the difference between the membership losses attributable to the invisible hand of markets and the visible hand of employer opposition. In fact, the number of employer unfair labor practices typically cited as the evidence of employers' visible hand of opposition fail to distinguish the various types of unfair labor practices unrelated to organizing, but are grouped under the same section (8.a.3) of the NLRA. Furthermore, the term, "employer opposition," has taken on such a pejorative connotation that it implies that all employer opposition to organizing is illegal, which, of course, it is not. In no small part, this can be attributed to constant repetition, absent qualifications about legal opposition to unionism. Significantly, Weiler, the harshest critic of employer opposition, acknowledged that "[m]ost employers still do fight within the legal rules of the contest" and that "our national labor law still states that employees can have union representation and collective bargaining if they want it . . . [b]ut they must really want the benefits of that institution . . ." Finally, it must be recognized that the magnitude of union losses in population and market share are too enormous to be recouped even if the union leadership had the will to make the effort.

The attitudes of nonunion employees toward unionism, that is, their demand for (or alternatively, their opposition to) unionization, is a more critical variable in determining the future of the Old Unionism. According to Freeman and Rogers, a large unfilled demand for organized representation—"a representation gap"—exists in the American workplace which they believe could be met by unions, works councils (euphemistically referred to as joint committees), or an undefined independent organization. However, economists have long distinguished between "demand" and effective demand, the former being a wish and the latter a willingness to pay for a product or service. The gap between a wish and a demand for unionization is demonstrated by the record of unions' continuing decline.

A fairly recent innovation in managerial practices which is an obstacle to unionism and may become more so in the future is employee participation programs. In response to increased competition, employers have established structures consisting of employees and managerial staff (at times) to promote efficiency. They are not intended to fill a representation gap, nor are they intended to address the terms of employment. Kaufman and others contend that there are representation functions (e.g., safety and dispute resolution) performed by groups which they term nonunion employee representation. I have pointed out that in the U.S., such representational activities violate the National Labor Relations Act. However, in a July 2000 decision the NLRB, in a three-to-two split decision, upheld the right of nonunion employees to have coworker representation in investigative meetings which may lead to disciplinary action; the decision is being appealed. Meanwhile, the NLRB has struck down some of these as employer-dominated labor organizations. Their futures hinge on changes in the membership of the National Labor Relations Board.

Why the Representation Gap Will Grow

The future will be characterized by a growing nonunion labor market. The same exogenous factors which have reduced the

Old Unionism over the last half-century will continue into the foreseeable future and, in fact, will become even more influential. Global trade will expand as foreshadowed by the extension of PNTR to China and its admission into the World Trade Organization. Employment projections show continued expansion of the industries and occupations in which unionism is weak (the New Economy) and stability or decline in those in which unionism has steadily lost ground (the Old Economy). Succinctly, the projections of employment trends also project that the Old Unionism is being left behind in the New Economy.

This evolution in economic and union history is understood by the demographic groups who are growing in importance in the labor market—people who are college educated and with higher than average incomes and who see little need for union representation. Moreover, as the organized system of representation has dwindled, a new system of representation, born in the 1950s, the individual system of representation, has evolved. Workers have increasingly found that the collective system has become irrelevant to their lives, while employers, who have always preferred nonunionism, have learned the human capital value of their employees and act on that principle in their dealings with employees. Thus, there is a demand and supply mechanism which motivates the individual system of representation. At this time, more than 90 percent of private-sector workers are encompassed by varying forms of that system. Should the employees' participation programs find general acceptance, legally and in the workplace, the movement toward individual representation will grow even stronger.

Other specialists in industrial relations offer a more sanguine future for the organized system. Freeman, after abandoning reliance on labor law reform and works councils, has recently offered experience from the years of the Great Depression a model, called the "bottom-up" approach to spawn a

new spurt in unionism: "The lesson from the depression experience is that bottom-up employee-driven bursts of union activity rather than particular laws are necessary for any resurgence of union density. Another lesson is that any resurgence
of unionism will come suddenly, probably surprising the current crop of experts and labor historians as much as the depression spurt surprised Barnett and other observers of the
period." Freeman's reference is to George E. Barnett's presidential address to the American Economics Association in December 1932. Barnett predicted a bleak future for American
unionism, just on the eve of the most momentous period of
union growth. However, Freeman distorts the circumstances
of the past and misreads the future. His analysis of the
"bottom-up" unionization of the 1930s omits any reference to
the virtual closing of the American economy to foreign trade
and the sheltering of unionism as a result of the Smoot-
Hawley tariff in 1930. He also omits from his analysis the successful illegal sit-down strike by the Auto Workers against
General Motors that the governor of Michigan, Frank Murphy, condoned, despite the illegality of the strike, which en-
sured its success. As a result, Murphy later lost his bid for reelection, but was recompensed with an appointment to the
Supreme Court. Similarly, Freeman omits from his "lessons"
of the Great Depression that the Steelworkers succeeded at
U.S. Steel because of the direct intervention of President
Roosevelt with Myron Taylor, the CEO of the company, who
agreed not to oppose the organization of the company, after
which Roosevelt appointed him to represent the U.S. at the
Vatican. Freeman also fails to mention the impact of 7(a) of
the National Industrial Recovery Act and later section 7 of the
Wagner Act (which organizers cited in telling workers that
President Roosevelt, a popular president, wanted them to join
unions). Neither does he make reference to the activities of
the War Labor Board of World War II which promoted unionization even more than the NLRB, as John T. Dunlop has de-

clared. Although a "bottom-up" technique was indeed practiced, its results were secondary to the "top-down" approach,
that is, the work of headquarter unions and federations
(notably the Committee for Industrial Organization, later the
Congress of Industrial Organizations) in supplying the strategy, the manpower, and the money.

While Barnett proved wrong in 1932, Freeman neglects to
mention the mirror image forecast of Sumner Slichter of Harvard who predicted in 1948 that because "[m]any kinds of
employees are organizing themselves into trade unions, and
these unions are the most powerful economic organizations of
the time . . . [and a] laboristic society is succeeding a capitalist
one." However, soon afterward the organized system's share of
the labor market plunged from its peak (36 percent in 1953)
and continued to shrink to barely more than one-quarter (9.4
percent) of that rate, and the decline continues. As Ferrier
wrote: "Why does the history of opinions contain such a list
of errors . . . but because men have so long mistaken their
conjectures concerning facts, for facts themselves."

The "bottom-up" assessment parallels the advice which a
group of academics (which incidentally also included
Freeman) gave the AFL-CIO on how to organize during the
1980s when the Federation finally came to grasp the fact that
unionism was slipping badly. At that time the academics' advice to the Federation was to enroll nonunion workers in benefit programs and to establish associations as precursors to
full-fledged unions. Neither approach worked; as for associations, the advice was premised on the success of unions in ab-
sorbing public-sector groups, groups which had been established a generation ago or earlier and could not be duplicated
in the private sector. In the public sector this was actually a
process of "organizing the organized."

The AFL-CIO has a diametrically opposite perspective on
how best to organize. In the fall of 1999 it ordered its state
and local affiliates to follow a top-down approach. The order

was also intended to increase the Federation's political might. Inasmuch as the Federation has historically been a minor player in organizing, its "top down" approach will be inconsequential in organizing. However, it should inject more vigor into its political activities. Indeed, the AFL-CIO is increasingly transforming itself from a trade union Federation into a political Federation.

Conclusion

The Old Unionism, organized labor in the private economy, is in irreversible decline. Economic and market factors beyond its control are principally responsible. The absence of effective leadership and its emphasis on political, instead of trade union, goals do not help. The substitution has diverted much of organized labor's large financial resources to advancing a political agenda which has brought no material gains in membership and market share, but stigmatizes the union movement as a "special interest" group and as the Luddites of the new century: "American labor organizations . . . are shaped much more basically by events of the past century than by forces of the past fifteen years."

The future of the New Unionism, government employee unionism, is different. Barring far-reaching changes in public education K to 12, the "privatization" of instruction, the New Unionism will remain stable, neither rising nor declining very much. However, because of that stability combined with the continuing ebb of the Old Unionism, the New Unionism will become the dominant wing of the union movement. In particular, the teachers' unions, the NEA and the AFT, will likely provide the leadership of labor's central body, the AFL-CIO. Their leadership can be expected to move organized labor further toward the Left politically. Its program will demand more government spending, the source of the New Unionism's power, and concurrently an even greater level of participation in political activity.

"*Diversification, experimentation, and evolution in what a union is in the modern economy . . . is how unions can survive.*"

Labor Unions Must Undertake Significant Internal Reform

Tim Kane and James Sherk

In this viewpoint, economic policy scholars Tim Kane and James Sherk blame organized labor for its own poor health and praise new government enforcement of union accountability regulations as a "powerfully rejuvenating tonic." Fiscal transparency will help weed out unions' shady accounting and waste, and unions will have to justify their political contributions once members get a close look at how their dues are managed, Kane and Sherk argue. Unions also need to change their basic philosophy, the authors conclude: The us-against-them mentality doesn't work anymore when the workforce is increasingly diverse and entrepreneurial, increasingly partnered with employers in stock ownership plans, and increasingly unwilling to allow unions to decide which political campaigns their dues should support. Kane is director of the Center for International Trade and Economics, and Sherk is a policy analyst in macroeconomics in the

Tim Kane and James Sherk, "Unions in Decline and Under Review," *WebMemo No. 1202*, August 29, 2006. Copyright © 2006 The Heritage Foundation. Reproduced by permission.

Center for Data Analysis at the Heritage Foundation, a conservative think tank in Washington, D.C.

As you read, consider the following questions:

1. How do new Labor Department filing requirements force unions to be more fiscally accountable to their members, according to Kane and Sherk?

2. According to the authors, what percentage of American workers say their employers are strongly loyal to them?

3. What three issues would American workers rather see unions address instead of outsourcing, according to polls cited by Kane and Sherk?

Organized Labor in America has lost its way. The most telling evidence is that unions have been shedding members for decades. It is time for Americans to ask why this is happening, not whether it is happening. A powerful example of how lost unions have become was seen during the [2005] debate over Social Security reform, when the AFL-CIO [American Federation of Labor-Congress of Industrial Organizations] and other unions fought loudly against President [George W.] Bush's proposals. Unions demonized all solutions aiming at solvency except one: an increase in payroll taxes. In retrospect, their argument was stunning—a direct call by a special interest for higher taxes that are paid exclusively by their interest: labor.

Other recent events highlight the peculiar dilemma facing modern American unions. The slow demise of General Motors (GM) is visibly intertwined with the inefficient labor contracts that the United Auto Workers (UAW) secured in decades past. Regular media stories showcasing problems at GM and Delphi send a potent signal to other U.S. workers that big labor's ideal business model is a bust. The AFL-CIO splintered [in 2005] when a number of major member unions broke away. Finally, the federal government has begun implementing significant changes to labor regulations. The Labor Department is enforcing accounting transparency in an effort to weed out corruption and bring some accountability between labor bosses and membership. That has been decried as an attack on organized labor, but it may instead prove a powerfully rejuvenating tonic.

The Paradox of Modern Unions

In the *Iliad*, Homer sang that "There is a strength in the union even of very sorry men." The modern experience shows the opposite can be true as well: There is weakness in some unions of very strong men.

The guiding philosophy of organized labor is that a union can bargain for higher wages and better treatment than workers could obtain individually. But the union philosophy sees the economy through a 1950s lens where only two agents negotiate how to cut the economic pie: management as the agent of capital and investors, and organized labor as the agent of individual workers. It assumes monopoly power for employers, lifetime employment for workers, and non-unique (lower-skilled) labor. Consequently, unions tend to prosper only in the rare cases where all three conditions exist—an increasingly rare situation in the modern economy. The economic pie is dynamic, and burgeoning entrepreneurship simply does not make sense to the union philosophy.

Why would a uniquely skilled artist, or uniquely skilled knowledge worker, need general representation? The new rules of the technological economy mean smaller firms and more individualized work, not assembly lines. About the only place monopoly power remains a reality is government.

What is most interesting about the union philosophy is its intellectual roots in 19th-century Marxism. Karl Marx famously saw the march of history in terms of a dialectic between two forces. But the forces of "capital" and "labor" were synthesized soon after the publication of *Das Kapital* when Great Britain formalized in law the limited liability stock corporation. In modern times, no one thinks twice about employee ownership of stock options, or of profit sharing, but they make the capital-versus-labor framework an anachronism. Entrepreneurs create capital out of nothing. They are neither worker nor capitalist. Yet economists who study growth now recognize that the entrepreneurial role is central—almost exclusively central—to explaining why productivity rises and why workers experience wage growth.

But the very things that big unions have been fighting for in recent years are hostile to innovation. They protect jobs of the past at the expense of jobs of the future. They fight for bailouts of inefficient corporations. They fight for higher minimum wages that price low-skilled workers out of the market (and out of competition with their members). Hostility to part-time employment, workplace flexibility, and capital gains are all antithetical to the virtual workspace that fosters start-up innovation.

In Decline: Overview of the Unionized Workforce

American workers have not remained oblivious to this fact. Over the past 25 years union membership in America has dropped dramatically: 21.4 percent of all workers belonged to a union in 1981; today, only 12.5 percent do. The decline of private-sector union membership is the heart of the issue, dropping from 19 percent to under 8 percent in just 25 years. In other words, nine out of 10 employees at for-profit companies are not in a union.

When the public asks whether unions are relevant, they are asking the wrong questions. Organized labor is very powerful politically, for now. But unions are almost totally irrelevant economically in the 21st-century workplace of individu-

Memo to Big Labor:
Innovate and Think Smaller

Open up membership to every pro-union American. If I want to support the women's movement, all I have to do is send in my dues to NOW. But to join a union, most people have to go through the trial-by-fire of a union organizing drive in their workplace. This isn't so in Germany, for example, where individuals can join a union whether their workplace is organized or not. Here, the Steelworkers have started opening up their union to unorganized individuals, but for most Americans the unions remain a distant, inaccessible fortress. Individual members wouldn't be just dues-payers and supporters; they could be the seeds of organizing drives in their workplaces. . . .

Lose those buildings. Big Labor might have been able to afford them, but it's unseemly for Tiny Labor to be sitting on hundreds of millions of dollars worth of elegant real estate in D.C., and I mean the Teamsters' building as well as the AFL-CIO headquarters. Sell off the buildings right now, at the height of the real estate bubble, and fan out into storefronts and church basements around the country.

Barbara Ehrenreich,
"Tiny Labor," Progressive, August 2005.
http://progressive.org/?q=mag_tinylabor.

alization and technology. There simply isn't any debate over whether unions are facing extinction, because the numbers speak for themselves.

Unions do remain a powerful force among one segment of workers: government employees. Some 36.5 percent of all government employees belong to unions, up since 1981. These numbers are highest at the local level, with 41.9 percent of all local government workers holding union cards.

The decline of private-sector unions coupled with the high rates of public-sector unionization has changed the face of the American labor movement. Decades ago the typical union member worked in the private sector, often in a very physically demanding job. He would strike to get higher pay or better working conditions. Today 48 percent of all union members work for the government. The typical union member nowadays is a local government worker lobbying city hall to raise taxes so the city can pay him more. Rather than striking to redress difficult working conditions, modern unions fight for more government because they are the government, drifting ever farther from labor's initial goal of improving the life of working Americans.

Under Review: Transparency Comes to the Union Hall

A new program to enforce fiscal transparency within unions by the Department of Labor is well-timed to help unions conduct a much-needed self-examination. For decades, big labor rightfully decried shady accounting in corporations, but never faced up to their own shady accounting. Laws dating back to 1959 require union reporting of finances, but until the Labor Department's Office of Labor-Management Standards began enforcing the law, very few filings occurred. That environment changed significantly on March 31, 2006, the deadline for filing a new LM-2 form that details the finances of any union with $250,000 or more in dues.

The Labor Department makes this next, union disclosure data available at its Web site http://union-reports.dol.gov/olmsWeb/docs/index.html, and a brilliantly easy-to-use Web site has been established privately at www.unionfacts.com/unions/. The new disclosures reveal exactly how union leaders have managed their employees dues. For example, the National Education Association has 417 employees earning over $75,000 a year. Seven hundred of the UAW's 1,209 employees have salaries exceeding $75,000. Moreover, UAW political donations are very unevenly distributed: Less than 1 percent of its $7 million in political funds were given to Republicans.

Those who support American workers can hope that the new transparency will foster the necessary change in the character and principles entrenched in union leaders. The splintering of the AFL-CIO may prove to be the tipping point needed to kick off some diversification, experimentation, and evolution in what a union is in the modern economy. This is how unions can survive. In that sense, more transparency and scrutiny are best interpreted as useful tools for rank-and-file members to reassert what they want.

Polls reveal that American workers do not see their workplaces in the negative light that union leaders do. A full 67 percent of Americans say their company has a strong sense of loyalty towards them.

And conventional wisdom is wrong: American workers are *not* frightened. Just 9 percent of workers fear their job will be shipped overseas. Moreover, workers are satisfied with their job security by an 82 to 15 percent margin.

What do American workers want? According to one survey, 62 percent of workers rated excessive bureaucracy as their largest barrier to job satisfaction, while 59 percent rated coworkers who focus on assigning blame instead of accomplishing tasks. In another poll, 60 percent of workers said that flexibility was very important to their job satisfaction. Unions have not put the effort into addressing these concerns that they have into fighting outsourcing, but these are the issues that matter to workers.

In this sense the discord among splintering unions is perhaps a sign of hope. For example, AFL-CIO chief John Sweeney is denouncing immigration reform proposals that would legalize guest workers, while Service Employees International Union boss Andy Stern has championed poor migrant workers. This is exactly the kind of diversity that will be essential for the union movement to evolve by trying different approaches to the challenges of the 21st century, not simply applying outdated approaches to modern problems.

> *"The American labour movement will have to partner with other social movements—peace, feminists, immigrant rights, and environmentalists, among others—and look beyond . . . wages and working conditions."*

Labor Unions Must Partner with Social Movements

Jeremy Reiss

Jeremy Reiss is co-project director of Urban Agenda, a research and coalition-building organization connecting labor leaders and other social movements in New York City. In this viewpoint, Reiss argues that the future of organized labor lies in social movement unionizing—broadening its focus to campaign for social issues that concern the larger community, such as health care, affordable housing, education, immigrant rights, and environmental safety. Reiss concedes that, as some labor organizers point out, unions are hard pressed enough dealing with "bread-and-butter" issues—wages and working conditions—and can't afford to spread themselves even more thinly, but he gives examples of New York City labor-social movement coalitions to show that so-

Jeremy Reiss, "Social Movement Unionism and Progressive Public Policy in New York City," *Just Labour*, vol. 5, Winter 2005, pp. 36–42, 44–45, 47–48. Reproduced by permission.

cial movement unionizing can both increase unions' power and give workers more reasons to want to join a union.

As you read, consider the following questions:
1. In what four broad areas does Reiss advocate union-social movement collaboration?
2. According to Reiss, what building legislation did NYC labor unions and environmental groups successfully promote by joining forces, and how does it benefit both partners in the campaign?
3. What did unions gain by participating in the TRADES campaign to train and employ NYC public-housing residents, according to the author?

Labour-community coalitions and shifts towards social movement unionism are part of a broad strategy for progressive public policy reform throughout the United States. Social movement unionism, at its most basic level, is the belief that in order to revitalize, the American labour movement will have to partner with other social movements—peace, feminists, immigrant rights, and environmentalists, among others—and look beyond its bread and butter issues of wages and working conditions. The notion is that global shifts in employment and changing national political ideology, as well as local challenges to organizing, have forced labour leaders (including the [John] Sweeney administration inaugurated in 1995 to lead the American Federation of Labour–Congress of Industrial Relations (AFL-CIO), the U.S. umbrella trade union organization) to re-envision and redefine labour's role internally as well as in relation to other social movements, locally and globally, in order to achieve its organizing and broader public policy goals.

At times, academics and trade union officials have been quick to romanticize where we stand on the social movement unionism front: unions, this view espouses, are championing both the immediate and long-term interests of working people, both in the workplace and in society at large, and are partnering with other social movements on a broad platform of social and economic justice. Yet in reality, as this research shows, the situation on the ground is much more complex. Unions, at times, do partner with other social movements. But respondents overwhelmingly indicated that, at times, these relationships are more "strategic collaborations" for single-issue campaigns. Issues such as wages and working conditions remain labour's core goals rather than goals integrated into a broader public policy strategy for progressive reform.

Social Movement Unionism in Practice: New York City

. . . Labour leaders agree that there are universal commonalities facing the entire labour movement: eroding wages, job security, and working conditions; decreased political power; and increasingly retaliatory federal legislation, and conservative local and state governments. They also realize, for the most part, that many local struggles resonate with the broader labour and social movement communities.

When asked to explain what a union should be, a number of interviewees responded that labour needs to find "the answer to the eight-hour day"—a modern rallying cry for the movement that can unite all workers, both those that are unionized and those that are not. One labour leader asked:

> I don't have the answer, I'm just posing the question to myself and to others: What is the equivalent of the eight-hour-a-day fight? What is the great unifying standard that we can say to all workers that we should be fighting for?

Goals obviously vary between labour leaders and between unions, but the majority of those surveyed agree that labour needs to broaden its approach to organizing and increasing power—by engaging in labour-community coalitions and expanding its list of public policy priorities to a) level the legis-lative playing field in which to organize and b) give workers more of a reason to want to join a union. Indeed, a number of powerful New York City unions are beginning to adopt these strategies, while leaders from other unions are pushing for this approach from within.

Such movement is indeed significant but can not be over-romanticized. Aspects of social movement unionism such as coalition building have been noted to occur in very top-down, bureaucratic, narrow, trade-focused ways when seen as neces-sary to win. Likewise, unions adopting a social movement ap-proach have successfully won organizing campaigns by pres-suring large corporate employers to agree to neutrality agreements without the support of a coalition or broader public policy reforms. Furthermore, as a number of New York City labour leaders proclaimed "change is happening but change within labour is always a slow change." Interviews showed that this slow movement is due to a number of rea-sons, including labour's reluctance to broaden its tactics, labour's hesitance to give up power (hence the frequent one-sidedness of coalition activity), the culture gap between labour and community, and the need for consensus within a highly diverse movement.

Indeed, movement towards social movement unionism in New York City and labour's role in a progressive policy agenda—to both level the playing field for organizing and to deepen labour's involvement in a quest for social, economic, and environmental justice—is slow and, at times, problematic.

Nonetheless, forward progress is focused on four broad ar-eas, each with vast implications for the future of the city:

- Advocating for the rights of immigrant workers;

- Linking job creation and environmental sustain-ability;

- Increasing access to health care; and

- Increasing access to affordable housing and the construction jobs supporting this industry.

The Role of Immigrant Workers

In moving forward, the role of immigrant workers in pursuing social movement unionism is likely to become increasingly important in New York City. It is extremely significant that while interviewees never were asked directly about the role of immigrant workers, the vast majority indicated the importance of meeting the needs of this constituency. One labour leader explained:

> I think the future of the progressive movement in New York rests on immigrants. This is the youngest the city has been in terms of new arrivals since the turn of the century and I think whoever gets to them first—and I hate to talk about them as a commodity—but whoever gets to them first, and addresses their issues first, that is where, at least for the next generation, their political allegiances will lie. So if you get them now—if labour unions get them now—start addressing their needs, both in terms of working conditions and also in terms of their community, then progressives win them, and they become progressives, and then we build New York. If we don't, then we lose them.

Another leader seconded this sentiment:

> As a city, we've also had over one million immigrants come in the last ten years. This is a city largely of an immigrant working class that we are not tied to in any meaningful way. The trade union movement, to grow and to have influence as we move forward, we have to think in terms of a broader movement.

The role of immigrant workers being the key to the progressive movement and the creation of social movement unionism is also well documented in the literature. But how to make this happen in a meaningful way remains an enigma, and is likely to continue to prevent social movement unionism from becoming mainstream.

Jennifer Gordan writes:

> The U.S. labour movement's ability to reclaim its roots as a social movement depends in large part on its approach to immigrant workers. A few unions, particularly on the West Coast, have successfully recruited large numbers of immigrants as both members and leaders. SEIU and HERE are the obvious examples, with others scattered around the country. But for much of the labour movement, immigrant organizing remains a puzzle.

[In the fall of 2004] New York City's labour movement took a big jump in broadening its appeal to immigrant workers. The Immigrant Worker Freedom Ride (IWFR)—modeled after the Civil Rights Freedom Rides—seriously raised the profile of immigrant worker issues and brought local labour and the immigrant rights leaders together to plan the huge New York City finale to this national event. While disagreements still remain in developing a specific legislative agenda to promote legalization, and while clashes of cultures caused serious hard feelings throughout the planning process and the event itself, the IWFR was a major step forward in bringing labour and community together to address public policy that can potentially increase union density and power—due to demographic and employment shifts, among other reasons—but can also provide the broader public with more of a reason to join a union. The IWFR itself, in my opinion, also served as a tremendous organizing tool for deepening and broadening the appeal of social movement unionism.

The IWFR created a model for which New York City's labour and immigrant rights communities could work together. Currently, a coalition is fighting an effort to revoke the drivers licenses of undocumented immigrants in New York State, regardless of their employment status, residency status, history of paying taxes, or their ability to drive. This mandate is being administered by the state Department of Motor Vehicles—an agency which has no ability to determine immigration status—due to pressure from the federal Department of Homeland Security, which wrongly claims that such a policy will make our nation safer (even though the rationale on which this theory is based—that only those with drivers licenses will board planes—is false). It is significant that unions and community groups are engaging in this campaign together. How they engage in the future will continue to shape the direction of social movement unionism. This progress has the potential to change the face and strengthen the power of labour, while also forging a public policy framework more supportive to the rights of immigrant workers (even amidst increasingly punitive federal legislation).

Environmental Justice: The "Blue-Green" Coalition

Since the tragedy of September 11[0] labour and the city's environmental justice community have become much closer, having realized that their visions for job creation, economic development, and environmental health and prosperity are closely aligned. Blue-green alliances have also increased in prominence at the national level with the creation of the Apollo Alliance, an influential coalition of leading unions, environmentalists, civil rights leaders, and businesses advocating for a serious public-sector investment in clean energy and good jobs. In our post September 11[0] world, this national security strategy for job creation in alternative energy markets has gained much political prominence and feasibility, if not with the Bush administration, then with the one that will follow.

These two factors set the stage for the launch of an official blue-green coalition in New York City in 2004—N.Y. Apollo,

Social Movement Unionism Is the New Buzzword

Social movement unionism has become the new buzzword for both the academic left and union reformers. As Ian Robinson noted, "analysts and activists have begun applying the concept to organized labor in the United States, as a characterization of some unions within the larger movement, as an ideal towards which organized labor ought to be moving if it wishes to recapture lost economic and political power, or both." An increasing number of people argue that social movement unionism is *the* strategy/ideology that North American unions should adopt.

Social movement unionism became prominent as an approach in the U.S. with publication of [Kim] Moody's book *Workers in a Lean World*. . . .

[Moody argued] that the changing nature of contemporary work undermines old union structures and practices and leads to a new form of unionism. The history of unionism has moved from "craft unions to general unions and, now, to some hybrid of the last two." For unions to successfully organize workers and mobilize their current members, they must adopt a new form of unionism: social movement unionism.

> Social movement unionism is one that is deeply democratic, as that is the best way to mobilize the strength of numbers in order to apply maximum economic leverage. . . . It multiplies its political and social power by reaching out to other sectors of the class, be they other unions, neighborhood organizations, or other social movements. It fights for all the oppressed and enhances its own power by doing so.

Michael Schiavone, "Moody's Account of Social Movement Unionism: An Analysis," Critical Sociology, vol. 33, March 2007, pp. 279–81.

which is a regional node of the Apollo Alliance. Convened by Urban Agenda, a labour-based research and policy organization, linking labour and community around issues of public policy [co-directed by the author], N.Y. Apollo is connecting labour, environmental justice, environmentalists, business, educators, and others to implement its vision for a strong economy and healthy city. The group is already influencing how the city is powered by promoting a framework that supports energy efficiency, economic development, and environmental equity.

For instance, N.Y. Apollo has been successful in developing and pushing legislation to promote high-performance, energy-efficient buildings and in helping shape a city-sponsored environment jobs creation strategy that will train workers—and thus prime the pump for further investment—in three emerging markets: high performance building construction, retrofitting, and maintenance; a green manufacturing sector to produce the products to support the high-performance building market; and alternative-energy markets (wind, solar, geothermal) used to power these smart buildings. Because it is framed as a strategy for maintaining global preeminence, N.Y. Apollo has been especially successful at gaining the support of the business community.

In addition to joining forces around issues of public policy, NY Apollo—through its inclusive approach that advocates for the environmental justice perspective to be integrated into all coalition activities—has pushed labour a little bit towards social movement unionism. A powerful political voice by itself, the environmental justice movement has also been strengthened on the legislative radar screen because of its central role in N.Y. Apollo.

Interestingly, N.Y. Apollo has attracted the attention of some of the city's more conservative unions. The building trades are interested in capturing the solar photovoltaic market while the utility workers see N.Y. Apollo as a strategy for strengthening the city's energy infrastructure. How and if these unions are interested in anything beyond their narrow self-interests is yet to be seen. The future of social movement unionism and labour-community coalitions as well as progressive public policy around environmental issues will be shaped by this question.

The Role of Affordable Housing

The notion that housing can build more than homes—that it can build communities—has helped reengage labour in one of the city's most pressing issues. For too long, labour has ignored the housing crisis, mostly because affordable housing units tend to be built by non-union contractors. However, demographic shifts within unions' rank-and-file and the realization that a new construction market could potentially be captured and increase labour's power have led to unions engaging in labour-community coalitions to create more affordable housing, and ensure that community residents get the construction jobs and are paid a living wage.

For instance, TRADES is a coalition of 25 public housing resident associations, labour unions (including the notoriously traditional Painters, Labourers, and Carpenters), and advocacy groups working together to expand employment and training opportunities in the construction trades for N.Y.C. public housing residents. The group is also seeking to a) increase the presence of union construction workers on local housing authority jobs, thus improving the enforcement of prevailing wage laws; and b) to repeal the federal community service mandate that requires public housing residents to provide 96 hours of unpaid labour each year, or else face eviction of their entire household.

According to TRADES representatives, the campaign grew out of recognition that creating jobs for residents on local housing authority construction projects is not just good policy but that it is also the law. A federal mandate requires that when federal funds are spent to renovate or build public housing, housing authorities and contractors must, to the greatest extent possible, hire and train residents to fill the jobs generated. But in N.Y.C. less than 1% of these jobs go to residents, and those few individuals who do get these jobs often receive short-term positions at wages less than the legally mandated prevailing wage.

For this reason, the group developed an agreement with the local housing authority around three main objectives:

- to co-operate with the trade unions to ensure that over the next ten years thousands of residents are provided pre-apprenticeship training and admittance to union apprenticeship programs;

- to comply with the federal legislation requiring that contractors fill all their apprenticeship positions on local housing authority projects with local housing authority residents; and

- to ensure that unionized firms have fair access to these jobs by requiring that contractors have state-certified apprenticeship programs and that they comply with prevailing wage laws.

This agreement not only set a precedent for how affordable housing will be built in New York City, but also for how labour will engage in this vital arena. Two additional labour-community coalitions are now working to address the city's affordable housing marketplace. One campaign is advocating that inclusionary zoning mandates affordable housing units for all new construction projects, rather than leaving private developers to choose whether to build affordable housing. Another campaign is demonstrating that affordable housing is literally built on the backs of an exploited low-wage workforce, and is advocating that the municipal government ends this exploitative and illegal practice.

These campaigns both address critical public policy issues—affordable housing and access to, and provision of, living wage jobs—and demonstrate that labour has a vested interest in engaging in labour-community coalitions to both level the playing field for organizing (by ending discriminatory and illegal wage and safety practices of employers) and demonstrating to the broader community that labour is trying to address the needs of all workers. How these coalitions and legislative campaigns play out in the future will seriously shape both social movement unionism and progressive public policy reform in New York City. . . .

Obstacles to Social Movement Unionism

Union democracy issues—most noticeably the fact that leadership and membership do not reflect one another—[are] a formidable obstacle to the creation of social movement unionism. One coalition leader replied:

> Our frustration with the New York labour movement is that the white males who run the labour unions are not going to give up that power so easily even though their membership is growing and growing and growing to be more people of colour membership.

Kate Brofenbrenner's research supports these findings:

> Exacerbating the situation is the persistent racial and gender gap separating union leaders and organizers from the workers being organized. It's true that significant progress has recently been made in recruiting more women and people of colour as organizers, but given the demographics of current and future union membership, the representation of women and people of colour among union organizers, and especially among union leaders, remains woefully low.

Another coalition leader went further, in arguing that trade unions will become extinct at both a national and local level if they don't address these issues:

Unless unions become truly democratic and reflect these interests, issues, and colours of the rank and file, they will not exist in twenty years.

Furthermore, a large fragment of New York City's trade unions oppose coalition activity. They see it as a source of distraction, leading to skewed priorities and declining membership. They also question why labour should always be the one helping the community groups—why labour needs to be the one leading the larger social movement.

One younger, senior political staff member at a private-sector union explained:

> If we had the market share we could focus on the larger issues. It is short-sighted of us to get involved in everything. We have an obligation to the workforce. From a labour perspective, it is just not useful to partner with the community-based organizations.

Another senior political staffer at another private-sector union echoed these sentiments:

> The question is 'when did it become labour's job to be heading the social movement? Isn't that supposed to be the democratic party?' At some point in the past, it somehow became labour's job to do this stuff and I think that is part of the problem with labour; we're distracted now away from the real bread-and-butter issues, getting involved in all sorts of social issues. . . .

Unions Should Not Miss This Opportunity

The state of social movement unionism in New York City has broad and dramatic implications for how these connections play out in communities—whether they create co-operative economies where labour and management work together to increase both productivity and neighbourhood sustainability, or on the other hand, whether they create conflictual economies marked by lower wages and weaker communities. The more labour and community work together, the greater chance that a movement spearheading co-operative economies can be created. . . .

In the long term, addressing these social policy issues has the potential to also address larger interrelated social, economic, spatial, and political problems such as poverty, social exclusion, and crime. Indeed, creating a state of social movement unionism clearly has the capacity to place social and economic justice issues on the political pedestal. But as this research shows, we are just beginning to walk this path.

| "Women workers are central to union organizing efforts."

Labor Union Survival Depends on Organizing Women

Kate Bronfenbrenner

In this viewpoint, labor researcher Kate Bronfenbrenner highlights a central contradiction of organized labor: As the proportion of women in the workforce has grown to nearly equal the number of men, the majority of private-sector union organizing campaigns continue to take place in industries and occupations where women are in the minority, even though union victories in both the private and public sector are concentrated where women predominate. Bronfenbrenner argues that 1) women are still hampered by wage and advancement barriers in the workplace, 2) women have positive attitudes toward labor unions, and 3) women make excellent organizers. Women can jumpstart the union movement, she concludes, if unions give women a genuine voice and leadership roles once they're organized. Kate Bronfenbrenner is director of labor education research at the School of Industrial and Labor Relations at Cornell University.

Kate Bronfenbrenner, "Organizing Women: The Nature and Process of Union Organizing Efforts Among U.S. Women Workers Since the Mid-1990s," *Work and Occupations*, vol. 32, no. 4, 2005, pp. 441–63. Copyright © 2005 by Sage Publications. Reproduced by permission of Sage Publications, Inc.

As you read, consider the following questions:

1. How have unions historically explained the under-representation of women in the labor movement, according to the author?

2. According to Bronfenbrenner, what percentage of union members were women in 1960? What percentage were women in 2002?

3. In which occupations is the concentration of women highest, according to the author? What percentage of these occupations is unionized?

The relationship between American working women and the U.S. labor movement can neither be easily described nor categorized. In part, this is because women's participation and experience in the labor movement differ so greatly across industry, region, union, occupation, and ethnic background. But mostly, it is a consequence of the inevitable contradictions that arise when the proportion of women in the labor movement continues to grow at an escalating pace, whereas for most unions and labor federations, the proportion of women in top leadership and staff positions has increased incrementally at best, even in unions where women predominate.

Nowhere are these contradictions more evident than in organizing. Although the majority of private-sector union-organizing campaigns continue to take place in industries and occupations where women are in the minority, organizing victories—through both certification elections and voluntary recognition campaigns—continue to be disproportionately concentrated in bargaining units where women predominate.

Public-sector organizing victories also tend to be concentrated among women workers. Win rates have been especially high in units with high percentages of women of color, particularly in health care, hotels, food service, building services, home care, and light manufacturing. As a result of these trends, women have accounted for the majority of new workers organized each year since at least the mid-1980s, and African American women represent the only demographic group where union density has been increasing. At the same time, membership losses in unionized manufacturing industries, where male workers predominate, continue to escalate each year.

Although the proportion of union members who are women still lags behind women's participation in the workforce, that gap is rapidly closing. If women continue to outpace men in new organizing efforts, whether by accident or design, in the near future the overwhelmingly male leadership of the American labor movement will face a membership that is majority female. . . .

Women and Organizing in the United States

Women are in the workforce today in numbers nearly equal to men. Still, a combination of outright discrimination and gender-based occupational segregation has left the majority of women trapped in low-paying jobs with few or no benefits or opportunities for advancement. Today, the median wage for women continues to lag at 77% of male weekly earnings. Although there are certainly structural and cultural factors that contribute to the wage gap, as much as a third of gender pay disparities are directly attributable to sex discrimination.

Although many women had great hopes that the antidiscrimination legislation enacted in the 1970s and 1980s would result in major gains for women in all sectors of the economy, it has become increasingly clear that labor unions are the only major U.S. institution equipped to help women overcome these barriers in the workplace. According to recent data released by the Bureau of Labor Statistics, unionized women earn an average of 31% more than nonunion women, and these gains remain significant even in studies where researchers have controlled for differences in education, training, and occupation.

Women and the Union Advantage

Today, over 6.7 million working women are union members and 7.5 million are represented by unions.

Many of the unions organizing in industries dominated by women, such as education and government, have consistently shown much higher win rates than those unions organizing in industries with fewer women members. The union difference is quite apparent when you look at the median weekly wages in predominantly female and consequently lesser paid occupations: union preschool and kindergarten teachers earned a whopping 56.7% more than their non-union counterparts, while for elementary and middle school teachers, the union wage advantage was 34.6%. In 2006, union librarians earned almost 29% more than their non-union counterparts, while union social workers and counselors earned 27% and 26.4% more, respectively. For RNs, the union difference was 15%.

Union women and men are more likely than nonunion workers to have health and pension benefits, and to receive paid holidays and vacations, and life and disability insurance.

Department for Professional Employees, AFL-CIO,
"Professional Women: Vital Statistics,"
Fact Sheet 2007, 2007.

Despite the growing number of women in the workplace, women continue to be underrepresented in the labor movement. Although the percentage of union members who are women has more than doubled from 20% in 1960 to 42% in 2002, it still lags behind women's actual participation in the workplace. Traditionally, this was seen by many, both inside and outside the labor movement, as evidence of women's disinterest in unions, with women being viewed by many as extremely difficult, if not impossible, to organize. Yet, for more than two decades, research has consistently found that women have more positive attitudes toward unions and are more likely to vote for unions than their male counterparts. By 1994, in her summary of research on gender and organizing, Marion Crain argued convincingly, "The once prevalent view that women are 'unorganizable' has fallen into disrepute". Instead, as our previous research has shown, women have made up the majority of new workers organized at least since the mid-1980s.

Employment and Union Membership for Women Workers

For more than a decade, changes in union membership paralleled employment trends, declining in manufacturing and generally increasing in the service and public sectors. Yet these overall trends fail to capture significant race and gender variation, within and across economic sectors.

Women's representation in the workforce has remained fairly stable since the mid-1980s, averaging around 48%. However, during this same time period, the proportion of union members who are women has steadily increased from 37% in 1985 to 42% by the end of 2002. These changes are even more significant for women of color. Although the proportion of union members who are white women increased from 29% to 33% (an increase of 10%), the proportion of union members who are women of color increased by as much as 25% during the same period, from 8% to 10%.

Even more striking are the changing patterns in the number of employed workers versus union members. Since 1985, the overall number in the workforce has increased from 94.5 million to 122.0 million, although the labor movement lost nearly a million members, dropping to 16.1 million by 2002. However, because so many of the membership losses were in industries where men predominate, between 1985 and 2002, the number of female union members actually increased from 5.7 million to 6.8 million, 300,000 of whom were women of color. . . .

As would be expected, the highest concentration of women is in health care and social services; public education; finance, insurance, and real estate; hotels and motels; retail trade; business and other services; and other public sectors. These are also the industries with the highest concentration of women of color in the workforce. Although both public education and other public sector are also the industries with the highest union density (33% or more), most of the industries with the highest percentage of women and women of color have very low union density, including finance (2%), retail trade (4%), business and other services (5%), health care and social service (7%), and hotels and motels (12%).

In contrast, the private-sector industries with the highest union density (18% or more)—such as transportation, utilities and sanitation, and construction—have relatively low concentrations of women and women of color. This reflects both the historical lack of union activity in industries where women predominate and, as we will discuss later in the article, the fact that current organizing activity has failed to keep pace with the rapid employment expansion in the service, financial, and retail sectors. Yet these data also suggest the great organizing potential offered in these industries, because women, especially women of color, are much more likely to vote for unions than men, and these industries are less vulnerable to global capital mobility than more heavily unionized manufacturing industries. The financial sector in particular, with 62% women in the workforce but union density of only 2%, has remained largely untouched by the U.S. labor movement. . . .

Regardless of industry, company characteristics, or even the employer or union campaign, unions have their greatest success in units where women and workers of color predominate. Yet, even in sectors where women are in the majority, the quality, comprehensiveness, and intensity of the union campaign remains critical to union organizing success.

Strategies and Tactics

It is clear from our research that women workers are central to union-organizing efforts. . . . Women are organizing in greater numbers than men, but it is also true that union organizing among women does not take place across all types of employers and occupations. In the private sector, organizing activity among women is highly concentrated in health care, hotels and motels, home care, building services, laundries, retail, and light manufacturing but almost entirely absent among office workers outside of academic settings. In the public sector, women are organizing primarily among home care workers, support staff in school districts, graduate students, and adjunct faculty in higher education. . . .

Employers do not act in fundamentally different ways in predominantly female units than in predominantly male or more mixed units. Similarly, most unions do not use fundamentally different tactics based on the gender make-up of bargaining units, but the unions that consistently use a more comprehensive organizing strategy are also those unions who concentrate their organizing efforts in industries where women predominate. These more comprehensive and effective union campaigns, coupled with the greater interest in unionization among women workers, allow unions to overcome employer opposition and win against the odds. But the effectiveness of these campaign strategies is not limited to units with a majority of women workers.

Although we found that unions had their greatest success in predominantly female units, greater use of a comprehensive organizing strategy would also make units containing a concentration of men more successful. Thus, we find that recent gains among primarily male workers by International Federation of Professional and Technical Engineers in aerospace,

SEIU in building security, and the United Automobile Workers in auto parts all depended on the use of a more comprehensive multifaceted strategy combining grassroots union building and leadership development with escalating external pressure tactics involving customers, suppliers, investors, and other outside stakeholders in the company. This is not to say that unions should ignore gender when choosing issues and tactics in organizing campaigns. But clearly a myriad of other factors—such as race, age, occupation, industry, corporate ownership structure, and the larger community where the campaign is taking place—must be taken into account as well.

In particular, unions must adapt their strategies to the changing corporate and occupational structures where both male and female workers find themselves. Traditional hot shop, site-by-site NLRB election campaigns are no match against large multisite corporations such as Wal-Mart, Cintas, Sprint, or Sodexho-Marriott. Instead, these companies will only be organized through national, multisite, and in many cases multiunion campaigns. . . .

Once Organized, Women Must Have a Union Voice

We also cannot ignore the role played by gender within the labor movement. Although it is true that unions are organizing disproportionate numbers of women, we also find that significant barriers continue to exist for women in the labor movement. Too few women are involved as organizers, even in units that are predominantly female. Also, too few unions use organizing committees that are representative of the gender and racial make-up of the bargaining unit. Perhaps most significant of all, women, particularly women of color, continue to be locked out of top leadership positions at every level of the labor movement, even in those unions where women make up the overwhelming majority of the membership. At a time when more and more unions are shifting resources from education and leadership development programs into organizing and political action, it is essential to remember that membership education, organizing committee training, and leadership development are core elements of the kinds of changes that are necessary for unions to organize more successfully and develop leadership more representative of the rank and file.

It is also important to remember that the tactics that are successfully being used in organizing today are part of a very different model of unionism—one that has a number of implications for women. Unions cannot expect to empower workers using these tactics during organizing campaigns and then abandon them once the drive has been won and dues are being collected. Although women workers and women of color are ready and willing to do what it takes to organize a union in their workplace, they will not endure the stresses and risks of an organizing campaign only to discover that they, and others like them, do not have a seat at the table, or a voice in the union, when the campaign is won.

Unions will fail if they see new women workers as pressure groups that need to be politically accommodated into the already existing structure and practices. Although changing demographics in the workforce may pose a difficult challenge to some unions, these new workers from diverse ethnic, racial, and gender backgrounds can also offer an opportunity to jump-start a more inspired, committed, and effective grassroots movement to organize workers in all industries, just as they did in earlier union-organizing struggles among textile workers in Lawrence, Massachusetts, in the early 1900s or during the rise of the industrial union movement in the 1930s. With these newly organized women workers comes an opportunity to broaden labor's agenda to include issues of discrimination, comparable worth, job advancement, hours of work, and a host of other social and family concerns. They also provide an opportunity to rethink union structure and practice, much of which was established in a very different social and political climate, to become more responsive to what is an increasingly diverse labor movement in a world economy where democratic, progressive, inclusive, and powerful unions are more essential than they have ever been before.

| "*Poor workers' organizing efforts have much to teach the labor movement.*"

Labor Union Survival Depends on Organizing the Poor

Vanessa Tait

In this viewpoint, journalist and labor activist Vanessa Tait argues that the revitalization of trade unions depends on a "bottom up" organizing strategy, that is, mobilizing rank-and-file union members to play active roles within and outside their unions. Tait urges the major American union federations, such as the AFL-CIO, to take advantage of the significant segment of the workforce that is low-wage and even unpaid in this effort. Historically excluded from union organizing efforts, poor workers have developed community and collective organizations of their own, and Tait believes combining forces is key to the future of the labor movement. Tait holds a Ph.D. in sociology from UC Santa Cruz; she is a writer and editor for University Professional and Technical Employees/CWA Local 9119 in Berkeley, California.

As you read, consider the following questions:

1. How does Tait define "poor workers"?

2. According to Tait, how do poor workers' organizing tactics differ from traditional trade unions' organizing tactics?

3. How would the labor movement benefit from unions organized along loose occupational lines instead of being specific to a particular worksite or industry, according to the author?

Although it emerged as early as the 1930s, poor workers' unionism started to take on its present shape in the movements of the '60s, spread nationally in the '70s and '80s, and by the end of the century had led to successful union organizing campaigns among tens of thousands of poor workers. Faced with the disinterest of most AFL-CIO (American Federation of Labor and Congress of Industrial Organizations) trade unions in organizing low-wage workers in the '60s and early '70s, as well as with entrenched racism, sexism, and bureaucracy in existing unions, poor people invented their own organizations and pushed ahead with campaigns on a broad range of workers' issues. Organizing experiments emerging from that era's social movements included civil rights–based job campaigns, domestic workers' unions, feminist labor groups, and welfare rights organizations. By the late '70s, community-based workers' centers had taken up the fight for economic justice, an organizing concept that spread rapidly to cities across the nation over the next two and a half decades. Community organizing, also booming during that period, became another vehicle for poor workers' activism on a host of economic justice questions. Just like trade unions, these independent community-based groups won pay raises, improved conditions, and secured dignity for their members.

Who Are Poor Workers' Unions?

People of color and women constitute most of both the membership and leadership of these poor workers' unions, which became the voice for a wide variety of workers—including low-wage service-sector employees (such as food service and home health care workers) and those with multiple places of employment (such as day laborers and domestic workers). Even "no-wage" workers, such as those receiving welfare benefits in exchange for work, have organized for their rights. From members of civil rights–era "freedom unions" who struck over poverty wages to contemporary immigrant day laborers who organize for better conditions, the struggle has been for dignity, social equality, and a living wage. Working independently of AFL-CIO trade unions, as part of a larger labor movement fighting for workers' rights and social justice, poor workers' unions illustrate a way of organizing that values the direct action, flexibility, collaboration, and rank-and-file control common in social justice movements over the bureaucratic and legalistic methods on which traditional unions have often relied. While smaller in scale than traditional trade unions, they stand out because of their unusual approaches to organizing and their commitment to workers' empowerment— valuable lessons for today's labor movement as it struggles to survive in the face of shifting economic sands.

Unions matter for all workers, but particularly for those on the lowest rungs of the economic ladder. In recent decades, the owning class has mandated increasing poverty for these workers, as capital has found new ways to exploit the low-wage workforce and widen its profit margins. Between 1968 and 2000, the U.S. minimum wage lost over 35 percent of its value while domestic corporate profits rose more than 158 percent. Disproportionately affected were workers in largely nonunionized sectors, such as clerical and service work, whose wages lagged far behind inflation. Globalization and deregulation, supported by neoliberal free market ideologies, have adversely affected workers' lives—both in the United States and abroad—as older sectors of the economy decline and newer ones emerge, bringing with them labor-driven migrations across borders. Many undocumented immigrants work in the expanding "informal economy" without benefits or a living wage. They constitute a huge and mostly hidden second-tier labor market in cities (in restaurants, manufacturing, and service work) as well as rural areas (in agricultural work). Estimated at 6 to 12 million, undocumented workers make up 4 to 8 percent of the U.S. labor force. . . .

Putting the Movement Back in Labor

As trade unions declined in strength, many poor workers were drawn into movements centered around race, ethnicity, gender, or community politics, struggles that occupied their imaginations and energies in a way the bureaucratized trade union movement did not. Civil rights demonstrations incorporated economic justice demands, calling for nondiscrimination in employment and fair wages. Feminist organizing articulated the "double shift" women worked at their jobs and in their homes. Welfare organizing sought to convince the public that poor workers were entitled to a safety net of income and benefits. Protections from workplace abuse or police brutality and help in organizing for better housing, for health care, and for other working-class needs came from concerted action among poor workers themselves, as they turned to labor organizing "in the movements," winning pay raises, social benefits, contracts, and dignity. To provide an institutional framework for their struggles, they built social movement—and community-based organizations with working-class agendas, demanding fair pay, affordable housing, adequate welfare benefits, and health care for all. . . .

Some of these activists formed unions independent of the AFL-CIO, like the Distributive Workers of America, or caucuses inside the unions like the Detroit-based Dodge Revolutionary Union Movement, or they got involved in coalitions like the Movement for Economic Justice or the National Welfare Rights Organization. These efforts showed that labor as a social movement was alive and well and living, in part, outside the AFL-CIO. Rejecting the narrow contractual focus and bureaucratic rigidity that had come to define much of mainstream trade unionism, the independents, caucuses, and coalitions expressed the dynamism characteristic of movement organizing. By the late '80s, some in the mainstream trade union movement had begun turning back toward direct action and community-based tactics, in part because of the influence of successful community-based poor workers' organizing. By the mid-'90s, tentative collaborations had begun between trade unions and poor workers' unions, primarily working on the issue of workfare and on living wage campaigns.

This history is at the heart of the ongoing debate about revitalizing the labor movement. It makes visible the histories of poor workers who, although they have often been seen as "marginal" to the economy and to many trade unions, have transformed the labor movement. Indeed, the marginality of some poor workers' groups has been one of their most intriguing aspects, lending them a tactical, ideological, and legal freedom often lacking elsewhere in the labor movement. These working-class organizations reveal a universe of activity that can broaden the vision of trade unions and the arenas in which they operate, as well as offer possibilities for collaboration that could strengthen the entire labor movement.

Despite numerous barriers to organizing, poor workers built on the economic initiatives of the social justice movements by organizing and joining unions of their own making. Many of these independent projects made progress under the same general economic conditions that led to decline for other parts of the labor movement. Why? Because their main purpose was, and nearly all of their energy went into, rank-and-

Reaching Out to 1.39 Billion Poor Workers

"More important than its role as part of industry or as part of civil society, the mission of trade unions is to be the instrument of working people to liberate themselves and transform their societies. It is not a question of what trade unions do for workers or to fight poverty. It is rather how workers use trade unions as their representative voice to demand their rights, improve their conditions, and express their views," said Jim Baker, Director of the [International Labour Organization] Bureau for Workers' Activities, addressing trade union representatives from 60 countries present in Geneva. . . .

"Collective action and organizing in trade unions are the workers' and the people's only tools to guarantee employment, decent wage and conditions, safety and health, social protection to promote international solidarity instead of selfishness," participants stressed, reminding that fighting poverty was the labour movement's raison d'être. . . .

"As far as poverty is concerned, trade unions and other actors face a daunting task. According to ILO estimates, 1.39 billion workers—almost half of the world's total workforce and nearly 60 percent of the workers in the developing countries—do not earn enough to put themselves and their families above the poverty threshold of US$2 a day. Reaching out to the poor, organizing them and campaigning for a fairer world is the task that trade unionists set themselves in Geneva."

International Labour Organization,
"Organizing Out of Poverty:
The Role of Trade Unions,"
October 28, 2005. www.ilo.org.

file organizing and democratic movement building, because they relied more on direct action and worker solidarity than on legal maneuvers, and because they targeted a population of workers hungry for organizing.

The Other Labor Movement

The labor movement is usually equated with trade unions—workplace based, contractually oriented, organizations usually affiliated with the AFL-CIO. . . . I use "trade unions" to describe this more traditional part of the labor movement, which is organized mostly by industry or trade and is employment based. But there is another part of the labor movement composed of independent social justice and community-based labor organizations. . . . I refer to these as "poor workers' unions" because they generally organize workers at or below the poverty level and they primarily operate within communities rather than in specific trades or industries. It is these supposedly marginal workers who are increasingly important in both the U.S. and world economies. Both trade unions and poor workers' unions are, of course, participants in the labor movement. . . .

Poor workers' organizing efforts have much to teach the labor movement. The way they operate complicates traditional notions of union organizing—confined to the shop floor, oriented mainly toward economic issues, and based on simplistic conceptions of class identity separate from race, ethnicity, gender, and citizenship. These notions were all hallmarks of trade union organizing during the '60s and '70s that still remain dominant today. Poor workers' unions fight for justice in the workplace and at the same time consciously challenge the balance of economic and political power in local communities. The framework of community organizing widened their struggles from purely employment-based or job-centered concerns, laid the groundwork for useful alliances, and narrowed the gap between employed and unemployed workers, women and men, and workers of different racial or ethnic identities.

The labor movement is now at a crossroads. It can only respond effectively to the continuing political and economic challenges of capital by creating new structures for collective action, or by dramatically transforming the ones it has, which are clearly failing. Weakened by its own internal structures and misplaced political priorities, and with membership at its lowest levels since the 1920s, the labor movement, according to the mainstream consensus, has been vanquished. If labor as a whole is to reverse its decline, it must build a broader, more democratic and progressive movement allied with other movements for social justice. Poor workers' unionism—with all its creativity, inventiveness, and historical variation over the last several decades—offers insights into that possibility. . . .

Inventing the Future

How can the AFL-CIO unions and independent community-based groups move forward with collaborative work and institutional transformation? While sharp differences persist between the cultures, politics, and structures of independent poor workers' unions and AFL-CIO unions, the potential for working toward common goals still flourishes. Trade unions need to acknowledge the organizing work that community-based groups have undertaken for decades. A labor movement that appreciates the uniqueness and creativity of this kind of organizing will tend to encourage beneficial coalitions. The democratic transformation of labor organizations can only succeed if trade unions and independent poor workers' unions communicate and work side by side, learning from each other and developing the ties of mutual respect that are so important to movement building.

This work must go beyond typical coalition building, in which one side expects only that the other show up for its rallies or endorse its campaigns. The Immigrant Workers' Freedom Ride ... exemplifies what is possible with mutual, sustained dialogue. A nationwide conference of poor workers' groups and AFL-CIO unions could continue the process, followed by continued interchanges among activists, mutual aid during struggles, and joint organizing campaigns. Community-based organizations and AFL-CIO unions have significantly different institutional structures, constituencies, and organizing cultures. But they also have potential affinities in their talents for one-on-one organizing and principles of solidarity. AFL-CIO unions often excel on the political and legislative fronts and can bring a measure of institutional and financial stability to organizing campaigns. Community organizations bring extensive experience in bottom-up organizing among disenfranchised and poor people, but they sometimes have a difficult time maintaining stable funding or long-term organizing campaigns. Joint organizing projects hold the potential to radically transform the labor movement by nurturing a different kind of organizing logic—one that builds ties of solidarity between all workers and emphasizes mobilization and direct action. If successful, it may also help trade unions transform their own internal cultures, so that activist community-based organizing becomes a greater priority.

Labor activists also need to think creatively about the structure of the labor movement. Harkening back to CIO industrialism, some believe the labor movement should pick its battles carefully and focus only on "strategically important" industries or areas of "core strength" like manufacturing, but in the absence of more expansive organizing, this approach might reinforce unionism's already narrow, workplace-based character. While partisans of industrial unionism have hoped since the 1930s to counter the exclusivity of craft unionism, they achieved only limited success with the alternative model of "wall-to-wall," industrial-style, workplace-only organizing. With industrial organizing tactics, union membership has remained concentrated in particular economic sectors and, as a result, is still effectively split along existing lines of race, gender, skill, and citizenship status.

A more inclusive strategy would focus on the large, growing sectors of the economy dominated by low-wage work. These sectors already account for nearly one third of all jobs and are projected to expand dramatically during the next decades. Cross-industrial, coalitional campaigns aimed not just at winning representation elections but also at building workers' power in the long run could dramatically improve the labor movement's prospects. If such organizing were successful, it would radically change trade unions into institutions with a more progressive social ideology, a much broader base, and even a different organizational structure. This new membership composition is already becoming visible among trade unions that have undertaken some of the more innovative AFL-CIO campaigns. This membership is not solely worksite- or industrially based but "organized geographically along loose occupational lines," as noted by Howard Wial, and acts "both as an economic pressure group and a social movement." In the poor workers' movement, where an ideology of social justice has driven its practical social justice–style organizing, this structure has already been in evidence for a long time.

To transform itself, the labor movement cannot limit changes to style and strategy; it will have to extend them to structure and constituency. Note Bill Fletcher and Richard Hurd, "As the workforce becomes browner and more female, issues of transformation are not limited to matters of technique and alterations in the bureaucracy, but must address the fundamentals of what constitutes trade unionism." They predict that union attempts to organize women and people of color "will not succeed on a grand scale unless there is a coinciding affirmative program to change the face and culture of the labor movement." The "cultures of inclusion" they advocate would explicitly confront issues of democratic leadership, race, ethnicity, and gender in the workplace and the union and, in the process, build unity among diverse memberships. Organizers and rank-and-file leaders need to do more than reflect the diversity of their membership; they must issue from that more diverse membership and maintain a foot in the world of the workers they represent. Poor workers' unions have long thrived on such a model, which builds real rank-and-file involvement from the ground up.

Actions Must Equal Rhetoric

Genuine change within trade unions, in other words, will require more than rhetorical transformation. Building a strong movement requires informed and active members. Winning the numbers game alone won't necessarily save the movement from decline—trade unions must take a hard look at their cultures of participation as well. Union democracy must advance beyond "democracy by consent," its current state, in which members have a formal vote but sometimes no real control, to authentic rank-and-file activism and control at all levels. Union strength and internal democracy are linked, as is clear from study after study showing that rank-and-file organizers build stronger unions. Top-down, staff-driven unions offer little to the masses of nonunionized workers who lack a voice in their workplaces and communities. Union members need to be more than troops to mobilize for a street demonstration; they must be activists integrated into the movement in all its aspects. They need to own their movement.

Finally, unions must put forward a vision of a just society, where workers strive not only for bread, but for roses too. This is what motivates all movements for change, but more than that—it is simply good strategy. Any special-interest group can vie for more resources for its members, but a movement with a compelling vision of a more egalitarian society can become a force for major social, economic, and political transformation. If labor hopes to become a new movement in the cause of economic and social justice, its actions must equal its rhetoric. Unions should prioritize issues such as combating discrimination, sponsoring fair tax reform, and securing universal health care, fair welfare policies, a shorter workweek, state-paid childcare, and affordable housing for all workers. Social justice unionism means moving beyond the bargaining table and into the community and the political life of the nation. It also means working for justice within our movement institutions.

Democratic social justice unionism, as practiced both in poor workers' unions and in trade unions, has done much since the 1960s to move labor as a whole toward a renewed vision. It is the brightest possibility for the future of the labor movement. Poor workers' unionists and their allies inside trade unions have kept this bright flame of possibility alive within the labor movement for the past four decades. They have engaged in an extended historical conversation with the rest of the movement about the nature of work, the agency of workers, and the possibilities for movement building. Whether the vision they have put forward will prevail is still an open question. In the meantime, poor worker unionists and their progressive allies will continue to build solidarity wherever they can in preparation for a future in which all workers might be represented. And they will continue to fight for their vision of a more inclusive, democratic, and powerful labor movement.

VIEWPOINT

"A new union model is needed to help the workers of the 21st century participate in the creation of the next social safety net."

Labor Unions Must Be Reinvented for the Freelance Workforce of the Future

Sara Horowitz, Stephanie Buchanan, Rachel Crocker Ford, and Monica Alexandris

According to labor attorney Sara Horowitz and her colleagues, 30 percent of today's workforce is working with a nonexistent or weak employee-employer relationship, without employee benefit packages historically provided by union contracts, companies, and the government. This growing, freelance workforce is cut off from health insurance, pensions, unemployment insurance, paid vacations or sick days, workers' compensation, and other social benefits. Horowitz argues that a "new unionism" should be developed to bargain collectively on its behalf. Sara Horowitz is the founder and executive director of Working Today, a New York City—based organization that represents the concerns of the growing independent workforce and finds ways for its members to pool together to qualify for programs such as health insurance regardless of their job arrangement.

As you read, consider the following questions:

1. According to Horowitz, what groups make up the independent workforce?
2. What percentage of the freelancers Horowitz surveyed were unable to afford health insurance as single subscribers?
3. According to Horowitz, what are the advantages of independent, flexible work arrangements over traditional employment?

Today's unions aren't keeping pace with widespread changes in the workforce. Our social safety net has become inadequate, while the workforce's ability to effect change has drastically eroded. We are at a moment in history where a new union model is needed to help the workers of the 21st century participate in the creation of the next social safety net.

Historically, jobs have contributed more than just a paycheck to workers' livelihoods. Employment provided many other elements of a stable, middle-class life: health insurance, retirement plans, access to government-sponsored social insurance programs, and an implicit guarantee that hard work and loyalty would be rewarded with long-term, stable employment and opportunities for advancement.

A New Unionism for an Independent Workforce

Our current employer-mediated social insurance system evolved largely out of New Deal programs built around an industrial model of work, with an underlying assumption that workers would be long-term employees of a single company. This employer-centered model of the social safety net simply doesn't fit the way many people are working today. In the face of competitive pressures, cost-cutting measures, advancing technology, and changing assumptions about the employer-employee relationship, employment is evolving into a variety of alternative and flexible models of work. About 10% of today's workforce is working without an employer relationship, and an additional 20% is working in arrangements in which the employer-employee relationship is significantly weakened.

This independent workforce—comprised of the self-employed, independent contractors, temps, contract employees, leased workers, part-time workers, day laborers, and on-call employees—is largely cut off from our employer- and government-sponsored system of social insurance. Though these workers have found ways to maintain income by adjusting to the changing economy, their work arrangements come at a price: access to health insurance, pensions, income protection, and other forms of social insurance is limited or absent. Without government or employers' help, independent workers must find their own solutions to manage these risks, or simply roll the dice and hope they don't get sick or experience prolonged periods of unemployment. . . .

In the past, unions have helped meet workers' needs by securing substantial employee benefits packages and important government social insurance programs, but union strength is waning. According to the Bureau of Labor Statistics, just 7.8% of private sector workers in the U.S. were union members in 2005. The independent workforce requires a new type of union to help address its challenges. 81% of [our] survey respondents feel that independent workers are a group with common interests and goals, but disconnected individuals can't create an alternative to our employer and government-mediated system of social insurance. Independent workers need a "new unionism," one based on organizations that bring people together to negotiate for necessary services and provide a unified voice for advocacy.

Independent workers need organizations to bargain on behalf of the group for affordable health insurance plans and other services. Independent workers need a unified voice to advocate for changes to a complicated tax code that targets them with additional taxes in some instances and denies them equitable tax advantages in others. They need education to help them figure out how to fund retirement entirely on their own while navigating an intricate landscape of plan options. And they need organizations to work with policy makers and government to pioneer ways to give them access to government programs and employment laws—such as unemployment insurance, worker's compensation, anti-discrimination protection, OSHA, and even transportation and child-care tax breaks—that don't [now] include them. A new kind of union can meet these needs, and in so doing, can help create the next social safety net.

Who Is the Independent Workforce?

Who are independent workers, and how are they managing—or not managing—to put together stable lives with little or no access to our traditional system of social insurance? Given the patterns of change in the workforce, their struggles, successes, and strategies may help us understand what the future holds for all workers.

In 2006, Working Today-Freelancers Union conducted an online survey of over 3,000 independent workers in the New York metropolitan area. Over two-thirds of respondents are self-employed as freelancers, consultants, or independent contractors. The remaining third work in temporary positions (14%), or as leased employees (3%), part-time employees (5%), contract company employees (7%), or on-call employees (4%).

Respondents are spread across a range of occupations and industries, with many concentrated in art & design (33%), media (14%), and technology (8%).

Others work in financial, business, and legal services; advertising; or fitness and health care.

Our group of respondents included people of all ages. Most are single (56%) and college-educated (83%), and a significant majority (83%) had no children.

About three-fifths of respondents earned between $25,000 and $75,000 in 2005. Approximately one-fifth report that they earned less than $25,000, and one-fifth earned over $75,000.

Key Benefits Lacking Without a Union

Finding and paying for health insurance coverage is one of the most difficult challenges independent workers face. Of those we surveyed, 39% lacked health insurance coverage at some time in the previous year. Of these, nearly half did not have health insurance for the entire previous year.

Respondents generally experienced gaps in coverage because buying directly from an insurance provider without access to group rates was too expensive (76%.) Four-fifths of these respondents avoided seeking medical care when they didn't have insurance. Some relied on public resources for medical care when uninsured: 22% visited a free or low-cost clinic and 12% visited an emergency room.

Without access to the lower-cost group-rate health insurance prices available to employers, many independent workers find health insurance difficult or impossible to afford. As one freelance event planner without health insurance wrote: "The government attempts to provide for low-income families, and of course those in the upper bracket can just pay for their medical services. But all of us in the middle must often decide whether to pay our rent, buy groceries, or pay for medical insurance." To maintain consistent coverage, independent workers need access to affordable group-rate insurance plans and seamless coverage that doesn't terminate when a job ends.

Because they don't have employers to facilitate access to group rates, independent workers need alternative intermediary organizations to bargain for these rates for them. In addition to providing access to affordable insurance plans, these organizations can leverage their relationships with insurance providers to advocate for their members' interests. In New York, Freelancers Union has been able to fill this role successfully for over 12,000 independent workers, two-thirds of whom were uninsured or had only temporary coverage before joining the organization.

Tax Burdens Are Greater Without Employee Status

Independent workers face complex and burdensome tax rules. They pay more taxes than traditional employees because the tax code overlooks them in some instances, and directly targets them in others. 50% of survey respondents cite the additional tax burden as a significant disadvantage of freelancing, and 94% feel that freelancers deserve more equitable tax treatment.

Some sections of the tax code directly target independent workers who don't have employers. As a result, these freelancers pay higher taxes than standard employees. The Self-Employment Tax—the Social Security and Medicare tax targeted at workers without employers—is 15.3% of net earnings. Workers who have employers pay just half that amount, and their employers pay the other half. In addition, a tax in New York City called the Unincorporated Business Tax (UBT) requires self-employed independent workers who net over $55,000 a year to pay extra income tax on top of their federal, state, and city income taxes.

Many employees have access to pre-tax financing programs through their employers to help fund health, child-care, and transportation expenses. These programs can only be set up through employers, and specifically exclude the self-employed.

The Shift to an Independent Workforce Is Permanent

Measuring growth in freelancing is difficult because it's not fully captured in government employment surveys. In 2001, the Bureau of Labor Statistics (BLS) found that there were 5.4 million contingent workers (those who say their jobs are temporary). It also reported categories that can overlap with that group: 8.6 million (6.4 percent of the workforce) defined themselves as independent contractors, 633,000 were contract company workers, and 1.2 million were temp-agency workers.

The BLS has not updated that survey. But economist Paul Harrington of Northeastern University's Center for Labor Market Studies estimates that between the end of 2001 and the end of 2003, self-employment increased by about 1 million, and independent contracting or under-the-table jobs increased by 1 million to 1.5 million.

Much of this growth has to do with the economic cycle, which recently has left many people unable to find the traditional employment they would prefer, Mr. Harrington says. But even as the economy improves, he says, a permanent shift is taking place: "This is a continuation of the way work is organized, so we are seeing a growing share of people moving into temporary and contingent kinds of work."

Stacy A. Teicher, "Freelancing in Your Future?"
Christian Science Monitor, *August 2, 2004.*

Temps, contract workers, part-timers, and others who buy their own health insurance policies can't take an income tax deduction for the cost of premiums unless their health care expenses exceed 7.5% of their total income. Independent contractors, the self-employed, and others who work without an employer relationship can deduct the cost of health insurance from their income taxes, but they can't deduct this cost from their Self-Employment Tax liability. While this discrepancy may seem minor on the surface, it can add up to significant savings for workers: eliminating it would lower their health insurance costs by 15%. These disparities increase the cost of purchasing health insurance for the very segment of the workforce already struggling to afford premiums.

Going Without Government Benefits

In addition to providing access to social insurance by offering health insurance and other benefits, employers facilitate access to government-sponsored social insurance programs. Payroll taxes levied on employers fund Social Security, Medicaid, unemployment insurance, and worker's compensation programs. The employer relationship also lies at the core of a range of worker protection laws. Laws that require safe and healthy work environments, or those that prohibit discrimination based on race, age, disability, or gender, do not protect many independent workers. Independent workers without an employer relationship can't access most of these government-sponsored social insurance programs and protections.

Unemployment insurance is arguably the most important program mediated by employers that is unavailable to independent workers. Unemployment insurance law specifically bars independent contractors from access to the unemployment system, under the reasoning that these workers have control over whether they are working, so they cannot become involuntarily unemployed.

Yet, many self-employed workers have a particularly acute need for unemployment protection due to the unstable, gig-to-gig nature of their work. 50% of respondents report experiencing periods of under-employment in the last 12 months, while another 37% report periods of unemployment. About 79% of respondents would be willing to pay something to be included in an unemployment system. As one respondent observed: "If freelancers were eligible for unemployment it would make a huge difference. Some months I have tons of clients knocking at my door and other months I can't find any work. The unemployment [insurance] would add some stability."

Traditional unemployment insurance protects workers from personal financial destabilization, helps them maintain spending during economic downturns, and gives them the opportunity to find employment appropriate for their skills. Workers without an employer relationship need access to some form of income insurance to meet these same needs, but they require an innovative model that fits the way they work. A system that allows workers to set aside pre-tax dollars for use as income insurance, potentially with some matching support from government, could help solve this problem.

Without Collective Bargaining, Freelancers Lack Retirement Plans

Freelancers face retirement savings challenges in terms of both access and affordability. Traditional employees can often expect some assistance from their employers, sometimes in the form of traditional defined-benefit pension plans, but more often in the form of matching contributions to tax-advantaged retirement accounts like 401(k)s. Independent workers must save every dollar of their retirement funds themselves, and they don't have access to a simple system of paycheck deductions and company-run plans to facilitate saving. . . .

Though they can't offer pensions or matching contributions, new intermediary organizations can help facilitate retirement savings in some of the same ways employers do. These organizations can pool workers together to lower the cost of professional financial planning help and to bargain for lower-cost retirement plans. Intermediaries can also facilitate enrollment in retirement plans by working with financial institutions to provide financial education and encourage practical savings habits.

Managing Risk in the Next Economy

In general, people like working on their own. 82% of respondents prefer their work arrangements to traditional employment.

Yet, despite their preference for freelancing, many respondents (59%) feel anxiety about their future as independent workers. This anxiety stems from an acute awareness of the delicate balancing act that characterizes the lifestyle. Success as a freelancer requires the ability to find enough work, manage cash flow to cover business expenses and hedge against slow times, plan for taxes and retirement, and find ways to get health insurance, disability coverage, and similar necessities. If one of these elements is missing, an unexpected event—such as an illness, injury, or even pregnancy—could be completely destabilizing.

Why do independent workers prefer their work arrangements to traditional employment, despite the anxiety and apparent risks? Perhaps some people are beginning to view the risks of independent work as less significant than those associated with a full-time job.

In a full-time position, a worker counts on one company to provide all of his income and benefits. He may develop skills that are applicable to a highly specialized area of work in a particular company. Essentially, his employer relationship mediates all aspects of his financial stability. Losing that job can be devastating. As employers' willingness to offer the implicit promise of long-term employment declines, and benefits packages become increasingly meager, the advantages of full-time, traditional employment seem to be waning for many workers.

Independent work arrangements enable workers to spread the risk of income loss across a network of clients or multiple gigs. Taking on a variety of projects allows workers to develop a diverse skill set and can help them avoid the risk of being so highly specialized that they can work only in one specific type of job or industry. Moving from project to project and building a client roster facilitates the networking that is required to find the next gig or get the next client.

Independent workers require new organizations to provide the social insurance typically accessed through employers, so that they can take advantage of the benefits of flexible work arrangements without sacrificing security. As one survey respondent wrote: "Working for big companies [is] less and less appealing. The only choice I see in the foreseeable future is to take our lives into our own hands. With the aid of a union that can protect us we can all make this happen to benefit ourselves, our children, and our children's children."

Independent Workers Are a Politically Active, but Overlooked, Group

Independent workers face a shared set of problems, and are beginning to view themselves as a constituency. 81% of respondents view freelancers as a group with common interests and goals. An overwhelming majority of respondents agree that independent workers need equitable taxes (94%), help finding health insurance (99%), simpler ways to collect unpaid invoices (95%), streamlined retirement options (93%), and unemployment benefits (88%).

Our respondents also vote in high numbers. 92% are registered to vote, and 90% have voted in a national election in the last 5 years. Many have donated money to a political campaign (40%), written to an elected official (59%), or volunteered with a community organization (58%).

Yet, just 3% of the independent workers we surveyed in 2006 feel that elected officials understand what being a freelancer is like, and 10% feel that the media understand.

Given the problems they face, it is perhaps no surprise that independent workers are significantly more politically active than the population as a whole. As a group, independent workers appear to have the qualities needed to form an active and influential constituency—education, participation, drive, and a real need for change. Traditional unions have lobbied for legislative reforms, organized support for political campaigns, and united their members around their common interests. The next unions will organize the independent workforce for similar battles.

Conclusion

Independent workers face tremendous challenges as they pursue careers within a system designed to support an older model of the workforce. These workers require a new system of social insurance designed to support the way they work. As employers continue to cut benefits like health insurance and pensions, traditional, full-time workers may soon find themselves in need of this new system as well.

As the workforce changes, and employers and traditional unions are less able to facilitate social insurance, a new form of unionism is needed to organize workers and provide access to social insurance. Many independent workers must handle additional challenges, such as complicated tax planning, recordkeeping, and business functions that are of little concern to traditional employees. These new unions can provide the additional services that are required to support new models of work. Moreover, these intermediaries would allow workers to access social insurance through democratic institutions dedicated exclusively to their well-being, thereby providing a platform from which independent workers can advocate for their interests.

The emergence of the independent workforce need not inevitably lead to a workforce that is cut off from essential benefits and employment law protections. Social insurance works because risks, like job loss, medical crises, or disability, are spread across a large, diverse group of people. The old model of delivering social insurance through employers and unions, in partnership with government, is inappropriate for this group of workers. It's time to develop a system—a new unionism—that fits the next workforce.

Periodical Bibliography

The following articles have been selected to supplement the diverse views presented in this chapter.

David Bacon — "Labor Needs a Radical Vision," *Colorlines Magazine*, Fall 2005.

Marion Crain — "Strategies for Union Relevance in a Post-Industrial World," *Labor Law Journal*, vol. 57, no. 3, Fall 2006.

Steve Early — "Labor Debates How to Rebuild Its House," *Tikkun*, vol. 20, no. 3, May–June 2005.

Peter Fairbrother et al. — "Unions Facing the Future: Questions and Possibilities," *Labor Studies Journal*, vol. 31, no. 4, Winter 2007.

Fernando E. Gapasin and Michael D. Yates — "Labor Movements: Is There Hope?" *Monthly Review*, June 2005.

Steven Greenhouse — "Labor Union, Redefined, for Freelance Workers," *New York Times*, January 27, 2007.

Larry Haiven — "Expanding the Union Zone: Union Renewal Through Alternative Forms of Worker Organization," *Labor Studies Journal*, vol. 31, no. 3, Fall 2006.

Industrial Workers of the World — "Effective Strikes and Economic Actions," *IWW.org*, 2005. www.iww.org/en/organize/strategy/strikes.shtml.

Marick F. Masters, Ray Gibney, and Tom Zagenczyk — "The AFL-CIO v. CTW: The Competing Visions, Strategies, and Structures," *Journal of Labor Research*, vol. 27, no. 4, Fall 2006.

Pamela M. Prah — "Labor Unions' Future: Birth of the Movement," *CQ Researcher*, September 2, 2005.

Terry Sullivan — "Unions Are Becoming Obsolete," *Louisville Courier Journal (Kentucky)*, June 24, 2007.

For Further Discussion

Chapter 1

1. Union supporter Chris Kutalik does not dispute Robert E. Baldwin's assertion that labor union membership has been in steady decline since the 1970s. How do Kutalik and Baldwin contradict each other, however, on the issue of unionization among less-educated workers?

2. How can the following adages be applied to Robert Fitch's portrayal of labor unions and to Lawrence Mishel and Matthew Walters's portrayal of labor unions, respectively: Lincoln Steffens's "Power is what men seek and any group that gets it will abuse it" and the proverb "A rising tide floats all boats?"

Chapter 2

1. The CLR Working Group on Immigration argues that the benefits of organizing immigrant workers outweigh the costs. Carl F. Horowitz argues that the costs outweigh the benefits. What costs and benefits do both authors describe? Which do you think are the most important?

2. Kate Bronfenbrenner and Stephanie Luce discuss the negative effects of corporate offshoring on U.S. labor unions. David Moberg discusses the positive effects of offshoring on foreign labor movements. Can international gains compensate for national losses, in your opinion? Use examples from the viewpoints to support your answer.

Chapter 3

1. Wake-Up Wal-Mart presents wage and benefit data to argue that Wal-Mart treats its nonunion workforce badly.

Christopher Hayes and Thomas DiLorenzo describe the tactics Wal-Mart officials and labor organizers have used in the campaign to unionize the giant retailer. Both authors portray these tactics as ruthless and unethical. Which actions do you believe are legitimate and which illegitimate on both sides of this struggle?

Chapter 4

1. Leo Troy makes the key distinction between workers' wish for union protections and their willingness to pay for those protections, and concludes that organized labor cannot reverse its decline. After reading Troy's viewpoint, do you believe the decline of labor unions is irreversible? Why or why not?

2. Tim Kane and James Sherk, Jeremy Reiss, Kate Bronfenbrenner, and Vanessa Tait all propose strategies for the revitalization of labor unions: internal reform, alliance with social-justice movements, organizing women workers, and organizing poor workers, respectively. Based on the arguments presented in their viewpoints, how would you rank these goals in order of importance, in order of difficulty, and in order of cost? Explain your reasoning.

3. Sara Horowitz, Stephanie Buchanan, Rachel Crocker Ford, and Monica Alexandris describe the growing freelance workforce as a disadvantaged group working without benefits typically accessed through employers or a government-funded social safety net. They argue that independent workers should pool together in a "new unionism" that would secure tax breaks, affordable health insurance, unemployment benefits, and retirement plans similar to those offered to employed workers. What social benefits do you believe independent workers should be entitled to, if any, and who should provide them?

Organizations to Contact

The editors have compiled the following list of organizations concerned with the issues debated in this book. The descriptions are derived from materials provided by the organizations. All have publications or information available for interested readers. The list was compiled on the date of publication of the present volume; the information provided here may change. Be aware that many organizations take several weeks or longer to respond to inquiries, so allow as much time as possible.

American Federation of Labor–Congress of Industrial Organizations (AFL-CIO)
815 16th St. NW, Washington, DC   20006
(202) 637-5000 • fax: (202) 637-5058
e-mail: feedback@aflcio.org
Web site: www.aflcio.org

The AFL-CIO, led by John J. Sweeney, is a voluntary federation of fifty-five national and international labor unions representing 10 million working men and women. The most powerful union coalition in the United States for half a century, the AFL-CIO has undergone internal reorganization since the 2005 defection of seven member unions representing 6 million workers to form the alternative Change to Win Federation. The AFL-CIO's publications include the biweekly newsletter *AFL-CIO News*.

American Rights at Work
1100 17th St. NW, Suite 950, Washington, DC   20036
(202) 822-2127 • fax: (202) 822-2168
e-mail: info@americanrightsatwork.org
Web site: www.americanrightsatwork.org

American Rights at Work is a nonprofit organization founded in 2003 that investigates and exposes unfair employer practices and supports workers' rights to unionize and bargain collectively. Fact sheets, reports, and studies are available on the organization's Web site, including the 2006 report *The Labor Day List: Partnerships that Work*, featuring profiles of union-employer partnerships that meet both workers' needs and business objectives and demonstrate that labor-management relations need not be hostile.

Association for Union Democracy (AUD)
500 State St., Brooklyn, NY   11217
(718) 855-6650 • fax: (718) 855-6799
e-mail: aud@igc.org
Web site: www.uniondemocracy.org

AUD is a pro-union, nonprofit organization that advocates a stronger democratic voice for union members within unions and works to defend members' legal rights. It provides organizing, educational, and legal assistance to union members. Publications include the bimonthly *Union Democracy Review* and numerous books on labor issues.

Center for Union Facts
PO Box 27455, Washington, DC   20038
(202) 463-7106
e-mail: longwell@unionfacts.com
Web site: www.unionfacts.com

The center, launched in 2006, is one of several antiunion groups formed by Washington, D.C., public relations executive and lobbyist Rick Berman, who declines to identify corporate clients or funding sources. The group attacks private and public employee unions through mass advertising campaigns and opposes the unions' campaign to replace secret-ballot union elections with so-called card checks. It charges that U.S. unions are corrupt, that they bully and fleece their members, and that they employ unfair organizing tactics. The report *When Voting Isn't Private: The Union Campaign Against Secret Ballot Elections* is available on the center's Web site.

Change to Win Federation (CTW)
1900 L St. NW, Suite 900, Washington, DC   20036
(202) 721-0660 • fax: (202) 721-0661
e-mail: info@changetowin.org
Web site: www.changetowin.org

Change to Win is a coalition of American labor unions formed in 2005 by a breakaway group of seven AFL-CIO unions who argued that the future of organized labor depends on uniting millions of new workers into unions (versus the AFL-CIO's emphasis on electoral politics aimed at increasing legislative and governmental support for unions). Led by Andy Stern, the largest CTW members are the Teamsters, United Food and Commercial Workers, United Farm Workers of America, and Service Employees International Union (SEIU). The CTW Web site maintains archives of editorials, articles, speeches, press releases, and position papers on a range of labor issues.

The Conference Board
845 Third Ave., New York, NY   10022-6679
(212) 759-0900 • fax: (212) 980-7014
Web site: www.conference-board.org

The Conference Board is a worldwide business membership and research network linking executives across companies, industries, and countries via economic data, forecasts, and business analysis. The board's purpose is to demonstrate the contribution of business to society through research on a wide range of business problems. It publishes research reports on topics such as workforce demographics and management-employee relations, along with the bimonthly magazine *Across the Board*.

Economic Policy Institute (EPI)
1333 H St. NW, Suite 300, East Tower
Washington, DC   20005-4707
(202) 775-8810 • fax: (202) 775-0819
e-mail: researchdept@epi.org
Web site: www.epi.org

EPI is a nonprofit, nonpartisan, pro-union think tank created in 1986 to include the interests of low- and middle-income workers in the debate over U.S. economic policy. Its fellows track trends in wages and benefits, union participation, and company performance; testify before Congress and state legislatures and advise policy makers; and publish books, studies, issue briefs, and other publications, including the biennial *The State of Working America.*

Global Labor Strategies (GLS)
Web site: http://laborstrategies.blogs.com

Global Labor Strategies is a comprehensive Web blog published by labor activist Tim Costello, legal expert Brendan Smith, and labor historian Jeremy Brecher, who present news and commentary on how labor unions, worker organizations, and their allies are confronting globalization. Up-to-date reports and useful links are available on dozens of topics, including labor and global warming, organized labor movements in China and Latin America, international labor law, Wal-Mart, corporate outsourcing, and global unions. GLS publishes books, including *Strike!* and *Global Village* or *Global Pillage?*, which is also available on video.

National Labor Relations Board (NLRB)
1099 14th St. NW, Washington, DC   20570-0001
(866) 667-6572 toll free • fax: (202) 273-1789
Web site: www.nlrb.gov

The NLRB is an independent federal agency created by Congress in 1935 to administer the National Labor Relations Act, the primary law governing relations between unions and employers in the private sector. The agency's Web site is a useful starting point for anyone interested in the history of the organized labor movement, how U.S. unions are formed or removed in today's workplaces, and what employees' legal rights are, with or without union representation. The text of the act is available for free download, as are many publications, including *The NLRB: What It Is, What It Does; The NLRB and You: Unfair Labor Practices*; and the *Weekly Summary of NLRB Cases.*

National Right to Work (NRTW)

8001 Braddock Rd., Suite 500, Springfield, VA 22160
(800) 325-7892
Web site: www.right-to-work.org

NRTW, a nonprofit group founded in 1955 with a 2007 membership of 2.2 million citizens, aggressively opposes compulsory unionism (mandatory union membership in order to get or keep a job) and promotes right-to-work legislation. Funded largely by corporate contributions, its staff and resources support four organizations: the National Right to Work Committee (lobbying, publication distribution, and antiunion-organizing activity), the National Right to Work Legal Defense Foundation (antiunion litigation), the National Institute for Labor Relations Research (research), and the Liberty Phone Center (polling and telemarketing). NRTW publishes fact sheets, state-by-state statistics, and the monthly *Right to Work* newsletter.

Public Service Research Foundation and Council (PSRF and PSRC)

320 D Maple Ave. East, Vienna, VA 22180
(703) 242-3575 • fax: (703) 242-3579
e-mail: info@psrf.org
Web site: www.psrf.org

The PSRF and PSRC, nonprofit groups jointly led by David Denholm, have campaigned against public-sector unions and collective bargaining since the 1970s, notably leading support for President Ronald Reagan's replacement of 13,000 striking air-traffic controllers in 1981. Their current agenda focuses on decertification of teachers unions and advocacy of Supreme Court repeal of the National Labor Relations Act. PSFR and PSRC publications include numerous antiunion issue papers and poll results available on the organization's Web site and the quarterly journal *Government Union Review*.

U.S. Department of Labor
Postal Square Bldg. 2, Washington, DC   20212-0001
(202) 692-5200
Web site: www.bls.gov

The BLS is the federal source of up-to-date statistics on the U.S. labor force. Its comprehensive Web site offers detailed information on workers' demographics, wages and benefits, union membership by area and industry, occupational health and safety, and private- and public-sector collective bargaining agreements. Publications include daily news releases and customized statistical reports, tables, and surveys.

Bibliography of Books

Sarah Anderson, John Cavanagh, and Thea Lee — *Field Guide to the Global Economy.* Rev. ed. New York: New Press, 2005.

Robert E. Baldwin — *The Decline of U.S. Labor Unions and the Role of Trade.* Washington, DC: Institute for International Economics, 2003.

Vernon M. Briggs Jr. — *Immigration and American Unionism.* Ithaca, NY: Cornell University Press, 2001.

Kate Bronfenbrenner, ed. — *Global Unions: Challenging Transnational Capital Through Cross-Border Campaigns.* Ithaca, NY: ILR Press, 2007.

Linda Chavez — *Betrayal: How Union Bosses Shake Down Their Members and Corrupt American Politics.* New York: Crown Forum, 2004.

Dan Clawson — *The Next Upsurge: Labor and the New Social Movements.* Ithaca, NY: Cornell University Press, 2003.

Stephen Crowley — *Organized Labor in Postcommunist States: From Solidarity to Infirmity.* Pittsburgh, PA: University of Pittsburgh Press, 2004.

Rick Fantasia and Kim Voss — *Hard Work: Remaking the American Labor Movement.* Berkeley and Los Angeles: University of California Press, 2004.

Liza Featherstone *Selling Women Short: The Landmark Battle for Workers' Rights at Wal-Mart*. New York: Basic, 2005.

Charles Fishman *The Wal-Mart Effect*. New York: Penguin, 2006.

Robert Fitch *Solidarity for Sale: How Corruption Destroyed the Labor Movement and Undermined America's Promise*. New York: Public Affairs/Perseus, 2006.

Robert J. Flanagan *Globalization and Labor Conditions: Working Conditions and Worker Rights in a Global Economy*. 3rd ed. New York: Oxford University Press, 2006.

Peter L. Francia *The Future of Organized Labor in American Politics*. New York: Columbia University Press, 2006.

Stephen Franklin *Three Strikes: Labor's Heartland Losses and What They Mean for Working Americans*. New York: Guilford, 2002.

Paul Frymer *Black and Blue: African Americans, the Labor Movement, and the Decline of the Democratic Party*. Princeton, NJ: Princeton University Press, 2007.

Julius G. Getman and Ray Marshall *The Future of Labor Unions: Organized Labor in the 21st Century*. Austin: LBJ School of Public Affairs, University of Texas Press, 2004.

James B. Jacobs *Mobsters, Unions, and Feds: The Mafia and the American Labor Movement*. New York: NYU Press, 2007.

Nelson
Lichtenstein
State of the Union: A Century of American Labor. Princeton, NJ: Princeton University Press, 2003.

D.W. Livingstone
and Peter H.
Sawchuk
Hidden Knowledge: Organized Labor in the Information Age. Lanham, MD: Rowman & Littlefield, 2003.

Miriam Ching
Yoon Louie
Sweatshop Warriors: Immigrant Women Workers Take On the Global Factory. Cambridge, MA: South End Press, 2001.

Michael Mauer
The Union Member's Complete Guide: Everything You Want—and Need—to Know About Working Union. Annapolis, MD: Union Communication Services, 2001.

Ruth Milkman
L.A. Story: Immigrant Workers and the Future of the U.S. Labor Movement. New York: Russell Sage, 2006.

Ruth Milkman
and Kim Voss,
eds.
Rebuilding Labor: Organizing and Organizers in the New Union Movement. Ithaca, NY: ILR Press, 2004.

Immanuel Ness
Immigrants, Unions, and the New U.S. Labor Market. Philadelphia: Temple University Press, 2005.

Silke Roth
Building Movement Bridges: The Coalition of Labor Union Women. Westport, CT: Praeger, 2003.

Tom Sito
Drawing the Line: The Untold Story of the Animation Unions, from Bosko to Bart Simpson. Lexington: University Press of Kentucky, 2006.

Andy Stern — *A Country that Works: Getting America Back on Track*. New York: Free Press, 2006.

Richard Vedder and Wendell Cox — *The Wal-Mart Revolution: How Big-Box Stores Benefit Consumers, Workers, and the Economy*. Washington, DC: AEI Press, 2006.

Hoyt N. Wheeler — *The Future of the American Labor Movement*. New York: Cambridge University Press, 2002.

Michael D. Yates — *Why Unions Matter*. New York: Monthly Review Press, 1998.

Robert H. Zieger and Gilbert J. Gall — *American Workers, American Unions: The Twentieth Century*. 3rd ed. Baltimore: Johns Hopkins University Press, 2002.

Index

Membership, union
  corruption causing shrinkage
    in, 41–43
  growth and decline of, 15,
    20–21, 41–43, 137, 139–140,
    161–163
  women in, 183–186
Mexican American Legal Defense
  and Educational Fund
  (MALDEF), 73
Mexico
  cross-border unions with, 88
  global unions in, 92–93
  NAFTA and, 64, 89
  outsourcing to, 79–81
Mexico Solidarity Network, 73
Military Families Speak Out, 34
Mill, John Stuart, 11
Mishel, Lawrence, 48–49
Mitchell, W. C., 146
Moberg, David, 84–85
Mondale, Walter, 140
Moody, Kim, 173
Movement for Economic Justice,
  194
Murphy, Frank, 155

N

NAFTA (North American Free
  Trade Agreement), 63–64, 89,
  141
National Association of Manufac-
  turers, 72
National Council of La Raza, 73
National Education Association
  (NEA), 142, 157, 163
National Immigration Project, 73
National Industrial Recovery Act,
  155
National Labor Relations Act of
  1935, 15, 151

National Labor Relations Board,
  54, 109, 121, 124, 153
National Restaurant Association,
  72
National Welfare Rights Organiza-
  tion, 194
Natural disasters, 34–35
New Deal, the, 203
New unionism, 157
  independent workers and,
    203–205, 213–214
New York City
  affordable housing in, 175–
    177
  blue-green coalition, 172–175
  building social movement
    unionism in, 168–170
  Council of Carpenters, 44
  obstacles to social movement
    unionism in, 177–178
  Unincorporated Business Tax,
    207
New York Times, 45, 108
Nicaragua, 106
Nike, 132–133
Noble, Josh, 121–122
Nonunion workers
  attitudes of, 152–153
  growing representation gap,
    153–157
  public employers and, 151–
    152
North American Free Trade Agree-
  ment. *See* NAFTA
Northwest Airlines, 30, 31, 34
No-wage workers, 192
Nucor Steel Company, 149

O

Occupational Safety and Health
  Act of 1970, 54, 56